In an age in which Christians are tempted to run, blend in, or fight, Jonathan Landry Cruse provides ⟨ ing us back to the paradoxical pat reminds us that true kingdom livir but in the Christlike character that
—**Scott Aniol**, President, G3 M

Jonathan Landry Cruse has given us an accessible, joyful, and delightful tour through a vital, if sometimes neglected, portion of our Lord's teaching: the Beatitudes. This is an excellent resource for study groups, Christian education programs, and personal study of God's Word.
—**R. Scott Clark**, Professor of Church History and Historical Theology, Westminster Seminary California

The Beatitudes are memorable and familiar, but what do they mean and how do they relate to our lives today? Jonathan Landry Cruse has provided a concise and timely exposition of Jesus's teaching that addresses these crucial questions. Take and read about glorious gospel truths for all of us who need to be shaped more and more by the glorious gospel of Jesus Christ.
—**Brandon Crowe**, Professor of New Testament, Westminster Theological Seminary

Once again, Jonathan Landry Cruse has written a gem of a book, aptly entitled *Paradox People*, because Jesus's followers live a lifelong paradox: They look poor but are rich; they appear forsaken but are loved by God; they seem to be overlooked, but their names are written in an everlasting book of life. What the late Philip E. Hughes said about the epistle to the Hebrews is also an apt description of this book: It is "a tonic for the spiritually debilitated," even for those who do not realize that they are debilitated. Take and read.
—**T. David Gordon**, Author, *Choose Better*

Returning to the Beatitudes is timely. While many Christians opt to run from the world, blend into it, or fight it directly, Cruse reminds us that the Beatitudes offer an alternative path. Christians are "paradox people" because kingdom life, values, hope, and the character of their King stand opposite the world's expectations. Through the Spirit, God will transform the world—not through politics but through conforming people to Jesus Christ. Reading this book will help you keep in step with the Savior as you learn to live on earth as those with one foot in heaven.

—**Ryan M. McGraw**, Morton H. Smith Professor of Systematic Theology, Greenville Presbyterian Theological Seminary

The Christian life is full of unexpected turns. The shape of the gospel—redemption through a crucified Savior—proves that blessing often lies in those unexpected and even paradoxical places. Jonathan Landry Cruse pulls on those paradoxes to show how the humble characteristics enjoined upon us in the Beatitudes are a surprisingly sure course to the blessed life. If you want a gospel-saturated guide through Christ's famous blueprint for Christian character, rest assured you'll find it in Cruse's excellent expositions.

—**Harrison Perkins**, Pastor, Oakland Hills Community Church, Farmington Hills, Michigan

Lively and engaging, faithful and clear, Jonathan Landry Cruse's *Paradox People* does what the work of a good teacher should: It points us back to Scripture. We find how wonderful the Beatitudes truly are: a royal gift from the King of Kings, who wants his people to know, no matter what we face for Christ's sake in this world—discomfort, persecution, even slaughter—that we possess the boundless love and favor of God, who triumphs through the cross. This refreshing and timely book is wonderful.

—**Zachary Purvis**, Professor of Church History and Theology, Edinburgh Theological Seminary

The Beatitudes offer a vital roadmap for Christian living, one that has never been more needed than at the present time. The paradoxical virtues of Christ's kingdom, to which the promise of blessedness is attached, are increasingly incomprehensible to a culture that loves power, prestige, personal success. With wit, clarity, and depth, Jonathan Landry Cruse's exposition provides a sure guide to the blessed life that Christ offers. May God bless this book and make of it an instrument to quench the soul-thirst of his people.

—**David Strain**, Senior Minister, First Presbyterian Church, Jackson, Mississippi

We are in danger of forgetting that we are a people of paradox, part of a kingdom that inverts this world's values, whose Lord is its greatest servant. We too often, as Jonathan Landry Cruse notes in this clear and refreshing treatment of the Beatitudes, let the world define the good life and engage it with a wrongheaded strategy of run, blend, or fight. Christ's kingdom is not of this world, and this should not prompt disengagement but wholehearted witness (even our being salt and light!) to the person and work of Christ, calling all to live as we should in this fallen world. Some self-identified Christians these days, especially certain younger men, seem to want to fight the world on its own terms. Cruse is one of a younger set in the church whose faithful proclamation of who we are as new men and women in Christ, which is what the Beatitudes address, from Christian humility and godly longing to Christian suffering and testimony, renews hope and encourages us all to live meaningful Christian lives, come what may, defined by biblical priorities—whoever we are, wherever we live, and whatever we do.

—**Alan D. Strange**, President, Mid-America Reformed Seminary

PARADOX PEOPLE

LEARNING
TO LIVE
THE BEATITUDES

JONATHAN LANDRY CRUSE

P U B L I S H I N G
P.O. BOX 817 • PHILLIPSBURG • NEW JERSEY 08865-0817

> If you find this book helpful,
> consider leaving a review online.
> The author appreciates your feedback!
>
> Or write to P&R at editorial@prpbooks.com
> with your comments. We'd love to hear from you.

© 2025 by Jonathan Landry Cruse

All rights reserved. No part of this book may be reproduced, stored in a retrieval system, or transmitted in any form or by any means—electronic, mechanical, photocopy, recording, or otherwise—except for brief quotations for the purpose of review or comment, without the prior permission of the publisher, P&R Publishing Company, P.O. Box 817, Phillipsburg, New Jersey 08865-0817.

P&R Publishing offers special discount rates for bulk orders and ministry purchases. To inquire about a special rate, please write to us at sales@prpbooks.com.

Unless otherwise indicated, Scripture quotations are from the ESV® Bible (The Holy Bible, English Standard Version®), copyright © 2001 by Crossway, a publishing ministry of Good News Publishers. Used by permission. All rights reserved.

Scripture quotation marked (NKJV) is from the New King James Version®. Copyright © 1982 by Thomas Nelson. Used by permission. All rights reserved.

Scripture quotations from the New Testament use the ESV's alternate, footnoted translation of *adelphoi* ("brothers and sisters").

Italics within Scripture quotations indicate emphasis added.

Cover design by Jelena Mirkovic

ISBN: 979-8-88779-129-6 (pbk)
ISBN: 979-8-88779-130-2 (ePub)

Printed in the United States of America

Library of Congress Cataloging-in-Publication Data has been applied for.

For Neil Quinn,
a fellow herald of the kingdom

and to him who became a curse for us,
so that in him we would be blessed (Gal. 3:13–14)

CONTENTS

Introduction: Kingdom Character   7

1. I Must Decrease   23
2. Weeping May Tarry for the Night   37
3. The Surprising Secret to World Domination   51
4. Satisfaction Guaranteed   67
5. Desiring Mercy   81
6. Devoted to God   97
7. Heavenly Resemblance   113
8. Through Many Dangers, Toils, and Snares   129

Conclusion: Paradox People   141
Acknowledgments   155

Introduction

KINGDOM CHARACTER

My kingdom is not of this world.

JOHN 18:36

We shall not go far amiss in saying that Jesus desired to awaken in his disciples a sense of the mysterious supernatural character, of the absolute perfection and grandeur, of the supreme value pertaining to this new order of things, and desired them to view and approach it in a spirit appreciative of these holy qualities.

GEERHARDUS VOS

MY FIRST TIME driving in the UK was a harrowing experience for my family—and the rest of the motorists in Edinburgh. Everything seemed backward and out of whack. The road signs were indecipherable, the lanes were too narrow, and, worst of all, everyone was driving on the wrong side of the road! Add the little sleep I got on the red-eye from Philadelphia, and the drive was a recipe for disaster. I remember shouting to my wife, after a double-decker bus zoomed past with its horn blaring, "What is wrong with everyone?!"

Of course, the answer was *absolutely nothing*. The other drivers were doing just fine. *I* was the problem. The bus didn't nearly hit me—I nearly hit it (and several others)! Here's a humbling question, and one we are resistant to ask: When the world seems messed up, could the problem actually be me? One thinks of the famous anecdote about G. K. Chesterton. In reply to a 1905 *Daily News* op-ed asking the question "What is wrong with the world?" he purportedly replied, "Dear sirs, I am."

There is no question that the world is a sordid and messed-up place. How is a Christian to respond? Or, put another way, how does a Christian individually, or a church corporately, live in and engage with a culture such as ours?

RUN, BLEND, OR FIGHT

Well, some would say you don't. Some would say you ought to run and hide. An increasingly popular view is that the only way for the church to remain pure from the defilement of the world is to remove itself entirely from any interaction with it. In this approach, the church becomes a clandestine commune.

Another option, perhaps, is to keep one's head down and try not to draw unnecessary attention to oneself. But this tactic can easily morph from a survival instinct in a moment of weakness to a full-out and unashamed campaign of solidarity with the prevailing culture. The flags and banners that an increasing number of so-called churches wave above their front doors indicate that there is no distinction between what they are offering and what the world is selling.

Still other believers have proposed that the days of winsome witness are long past and that now is the time for action and retaliation. The world must be conquered for Christ—and by force. We see this play out in uncompromising stances pushed on social media, generally bolstered by crass language and hostility to any who take opposing views. Theirs is a reductionistic worldview that makes no room for nuance, compassion, or discernment—the state of society proves that it is far too late for such things, they would argue.

Though these three are each quite different approaches—run, blend, or fight—there is something that unites them: They operate under the principle that the world is the primary problem. But in thinking through how the Christian relates to culture, I wonder if that puts the focus on the wrong place. Perhaps there is much wisdom in the Chestertonian perspective: *I am wrong.* The issue that should concern us most is not that we are *in* the world but that we are all too often *like* the world (see John 17:15–16).

A similar theme emerges in Jesus's magnificent discourse known as the Sermon on the Mount (see Matt. 5–7). Its great theme is that of life in the kingdom of God. How do we know? Beyond the eight explicit references to "kingdom" in the sermon itself, Matthew summarizes Christ's preaching with the proclamation "Repent, for the kingdom of heaven is at hand" (4:17) and describes his public ministry this way: "And he went throughout all Galilee, teaching in their synagogues and proclaiming [*kerusso*; 'preaching'] the gospel of the kingdom and healing every disease and every affliction among the people" (4:23). Yet in this sermon on kingdom living, he doesn't say anything about running from the world, blending into it, or taking up arms against it. Instead, he talks about holiness. He talks about character. He talks about virtue. He talks about what is true for those who are holy and righteous by virtue of their union with him, and he calls us all to live out that internal reality. Bishop J. C. Ryle once wrote, "Would we know what kind of people Christians ought to be? Would we know the character at which Christians ought to aim? . . . Then let us often study the Sermon on the Mount. Let us often ponder each sentence, and prove ourselves by it."[1] Wise counsel, and the very aim of this little book.

INTRODUCING THE BEATITUDES

In this book, we will not consider the entirety of Jesus's sermon but simply consider his introduction to it. Jesus opens not with a personal illustration or a humorous anecdote but with a series of incisive, memorable aphorisms on kingdom character known as the Beatitudes. This term comes from the Latin *beatitudo*, which means "blessedness." Each beatitude promises a blessing to the citizen of God's kingdom who bears a particular character trait, after which Jesus briefly explicates what the blessing is. Interestingly, the first and last blessings on the list are the

---

1. J. C. Ryle, *Matthew: Expository Thoughts on the Gospels* (repr., Banner of Truth, 2012), 26.

exact same: "... for theirs is the kingdom of heaven" (vv. 3, 10). This is a literary device known as an *inclusio*, something that acts as bookends informing the reader that everything *included* in the middle should be interpreted through the meaning of the bookends. So, in this context, the *inclusio* means that all the Beatitudes are teaching the blessedness of belonging to the kingdom of heaven.[2]

The rest of the sermon unpacks some of the particulars of kingdom living: what it means for our finances, marriages, or civil disputes, for example. But before all that, Jesus makes it abundantly (and mercifully!) simple for us. It's as though he says, "Do you want to know what it looks like to live in the kingdom of God? It looks like this . . ." Then he describes eight characteristics of kingdom citizens, concluding with two further metaphorical attributes:[3]

> Blessed are the poor in spirit, for theirs is the kingdom of heaven. (Matt. 5:3)
>
> Blessed are those who mourn, for they shall be comforted. (v. 4)
>
> Blessed are the meek, for they shall inherit the earth. (v. 5)
>
> Blessed are those who hunger and thirst for righteousness, for they shall be satisfied. (v. 6)
>
> Blessed are the merciful, for they shall receive mercy. (v. 7)

---

2. See D. A. Carson, *Jesus's Sermon on the Mount and His Confrontation with the World: A Study of Matthew 5–10* (repr., Baker Books, 2018), 20.

3. Some interpreters suggest a total of nine beatitudes, as Jesus declares "Blessed are . . ." nine times. For the purposes of this study, I will be taking verses 10–12 together, with 11–12 serving as a further elaboration of the beatitude "Blessed are those who are persecuted." See R. T. France, *The Gospel of Matthew*, New International Commentary on the New Testament (Eerdmans, 2007), 161n13.

Blessed are the pure in heart, for they shall see God. (v. 8)

Blessed are the peacemakers, for they shall be called sons of God. (v. 9)

Blessed are those who are persecuted for righteousness' sake, for theirs is the kingdom of heaven. (v. 10)

Blessed are you when others revile you and persecute you and utter all kinds of evil against you falsely on my account. Rejoice and be glad, for your reward is great in heaven, for so they persecuted the prophets who were before you. (vv. 11–12)

You are the salt of the earth, but if salt has lost its taste, how shall its saltiness be restored? It is no longer good for anything except to be thrown out and trampled under people's feet. (v. 13)

You are the light of the world. A city set on a hill cannot be hidden. Nor do people light a lamp and put it under a basket, but on a stand, and it gives light to all in the house. In the same way, let your light shine before others, so that they may see your good works and give glory to your Father who is in heaven. (vv. 14–16)

KINGDOM LIFE PICTURED

What should become immediately evident is that living in God's kingdom looks very different from living in man's kingdom. Jesus rhetorically establishes an antithesis between the world and the church through the repeated use of "theirs," implying that the blessing that belongs to the church is kept from the world. It is as though he said, "Theirs is the kingdom of God, and theirs only. No one else's."

The difference between the Christian and the non-Christian is "the vital thing that is emphasized everywhere in this passage," said the great preacher Martyn Lloyd-Jones. Writing in the 1950s, he claimed that "the first need in the Church is a clear understanding of this essential difference" and that the Sermon on the Mount was one of the best aids to that end.[4] Things haven't changed since then—in fact, things have never changed. Jesus climbed on the mount to deliver an address calling God's people to live different lives than the rest of the world. Over a thousand years earlier, another prophet named Moses did something quite similar.[5] Although there were many differences between the two prophets and their preaching, they sounded the same heavenly call: "You shall be holy to me, for I the LORD am holy and have separated you from the peoples, that you should be mine" (Lev. 20:26).

So, in what ways is life in God's kingdom pictured differently from life in man's kingdom? At least three things should be noted: Christians must be distinguished from the world by their values, their hopes, and, ultimately, their King.

The Kingdom's Value System

Right away, we see that the Beatitudes praise and favor what the world mocks and shames. What's so great about being "poor in spirit," after all? Mourning, meekness, and mercy are not rungs on the ladder of the corporate world. Nevertheless, these are what Jesus commends to us when describing kingdom life. Notice, he is

---

4. D. Martyn Lloyd-Jones, *Studies in the Sermon on the Mount* (repr., Eerdmans, 1987), 39.

5. See Thomas R. Schreiner, *New Testament Theology: Magnifying God in Christ* (Baker Academic, 2008), 173–75; and Jonathan T. Pennington, *The Sermon on the Mount and Human Flourishing: A Theological Commentary* (Baker Academic, 2017), 137–43.

not saying those who are poor, or mourning, or meek, or hungry will be blessed *because* they are so pathetic and wretched. He is saying they are blessed because their values align with his. He is not pitying such people but presenting them as examples! These are values the world criticizes, but Christ catapults them to the highest degrees of honor.[6]

Be that as it may, admittedly, it all seems sort of upside-down at first. It can be hard to approach the teaching of the kingdom of heaven with appreciation. It's difficult to "reconcile the blessedness we seek with the idea of shame, poverty, hunger, thirst, and other such afflictions," as John Calvin so honestly writes.[7] We are to be a people who pursue paradox: The values that we are called to won't seem natural to us—at times they might seem outright foolish—but blessing is found not by railing against them but by wholeheartedly embracing them. It's like when I was driving in Scotland: It was not until I accepted rules that were nonsensical to me that I found I could get around. Whether we fully understand it or not, there is, in the words of one Puritan, "blessedness in reversions."[8] Christianity is an otherworldly religion—so we should not be surprised when it turns us and others upside down (see Acts 17:6).

The Kingdom's Hope

The hope that a Christian has is ultimately not in this world; this is indicated by the fact that all but the first and last beatitudes promise a blessing that is ultimately reserved for a later time. The mourners *will* be comforted, the hungry *will* be satisfied, the pure

---

6. See Geerhardus Vos, *The Teaching of Jesus Concerning the Kingdom of God and the Church* (repr., Fontes Press, 2017), 18.
7. John Calvin, *Sermons on the Beatitudes* (Banner of Truth, 2006), 19.
8. Thomas Watson, *The Beatitudes: An Exposition of Matthew 5:1–10* (repr., Banner of Truth, 1980), 24.

will see God. At the same time, the controlling theme of the Beatitudes is that those who are blessed have the kingdom of heaven right now (see vv. 3, 10). The Christian lives as one between the times, as it were. Theirs is the kingdom of heaven because the regenerating power of God has come into their lives, even though all the blessings that attend this transformation have not yet been realized (see 1 Peter 1:3–5). "If anyone is in Christ, he is a new creation" (2 Cor. 5:17); but he is not yet *in* the new creation.

The Beatitudes help us look somewhere other than the here and now for our comfort and consolation. Unlike the world, our hope is not in the next paycheck, the next vacation, or the next spouse. The faithful Christian says with Paul, "For who hopes for what he sees? But if we hope for what we do not see, we wait for it with patience" (Rom. 8:24–25).

The Kingdom's King

The key to the kingdom, however, is the King. The Beatitudes handed down from the mount matter because of the One who ascended the mount. Indeed, they are a portrait of him. Throughout his life on earth, Jesus was poor in spirit (see Phil. 2:8), he mourned (see Matt. 26:38), he was meek (see Matt. 11:29), he hungered after God (see Matt. 4:4), he was merciful (see Luke 17:13–14), he was pure in heart (see Matt. 4:10), he made peace (see John 14:27), and he was persecuted (see 1 Peter 2:23)—and on account of these things he has received the blessing of the kingdom of God, having been appointed "the heir of all things" (Heb. 1:2).[9] It is impossible to have a proper understanding of the Beatitudes without having a proper understanding of Christ, for there is no blessing apart from

---

9. For a wonderful treatment of Christ as the fulfillment of the virtues listed in the Beatitudes, see Iain M. Duguid, *Hero of Heroes: Seeing Christ in the Beatitudes* (P&R, 2001).

him. The King is the greatest kingdom blessing. The call to live in God's kingdom is a call to live before *this* King—and he is very different from any other the world has ever seen (see John 18:36).

In recent years, there's been a surge in shows centered on so-called "antiheroes"—protagonists who lack the classic virtues of heroism, such as courage, idealism, or moral integrity. Unlike traditional heroes who fight for justice, antiheroes are often cynical, flawed, and morally ambiguous—yet they still manage to earn our sympathy or admiration. Their rise in popularity says something sobering about our culture. What kind of heroes do we really admire? Those who mirror our own flaws and justify our sinful tendencies? Or those who are so radically virtuous that they call us to something higher?

Jesus is a hero in the classic sense—fighting the ultimate battle between good and evil. Yet his methods make him seem like an antihero, not because he does wrong but because he defies our expectations. He finds strength in weakness, values humility over power, refuses to defend himself, seeks no personal gain, and aligns himself with the outcasts of society. Our response to him reveals the state of our hearts. Do we love a hero like this? Kingdom living demands it.

KINGDOM LIFE PROMISED

The opening salvo of this New Moses's sermon is not a list of unattainable qualities but rather the declaration that God has made these things true of us and in us. Jesus "is describing *what the power of God's kingdom makes us*," writes Sinclair Ferguson.[10]

---

10. Sinclair B. Ferguson, *The Sermon on the Mount: Kingdom Life in a Fallen World* (repr., Banner of Truth, 2009), 44. Emphasis original.

Therefore, in the Beatitudes we find kingdom life not only pictured but also promised! The anti-Beatitudes are found in Matthew 23, where Jesus declares "woes" upon the people of Israel who have rejected their God. For the Christian, the one who embraces God, life is not woeful. It is full of blessing. The gospel wondrously declares to us that we stand in God's favor. And this is not because we have earned it; it's because Christ has.

How could sinners such as us receive divine favor and approval? Only through union with the One who has found ultimate approval from God. Flip back a page in your Bible, and you will find that Matthew has told us who this is: "This is my beloved Son, with whom I am well pleased" (Matt. 3:17). The Beatitudes make sense only when viewed through a gospel lens. They are not goals for us to achieve but blessings we receive when we belong to the One who perfectly fulfilled all righteousness for us. And when we are in Christ, we are in him perfectly, completely, unshakably. We stand in the favor of God forever.

This is the best way to understand the "blessedness" of these blessings. It is the objective fact that no matter what happens in life, God is for us. This divine favor produces a state of being that Jesus refers to as utter blessedness. Some translations render the word *blessed* (*makarios*) as "happy." This helps convey the good life that the Beatitudes usher us into. Perhaps more helpful still (and definitely more interesting!) is the Welsh rendering of the Beatitudes, which uses the idiom *Gwyn ey byd*—literally, "white is their world"—which succinctly portrays the pristine, contented life of those who belong to Christ's kingdom. But we need to be cautious here, because the concepts of happiness and flourishing are very *subjective*, whereas the Beatitudes are largely concerned with the *objective* favor we have from God. In other words, they teach, in part, that our happiness and wholeness and flourishing can come only from God's favor and approval.

That's what the *very first* beatitude declares, after all: Even when we have seemingly nothing ("poor in spirit"), we have absolutely everything ("the kingdom of heaven"). The gospel finds us impoverished in sin and promises that we will be filled with the very fullness of God (see John 1:16). All we have to do is believe it. We might not see it in this life. Again, we remember that most of the blessings are held out for us in the future world yet to come. But even this is gospel security. As R. V. G. Tasker helpfully explained, "The future tense . . . emphasizes their certainty and not merely their futurity."[11] We could put an *indeed* before each future blessing—and let's underscore it while we're at it: "Blessed are those who mourn, for they shall *indeed* be comforted" (v. 4). Don't sense the gospel promise yet? How about this: "Blessed are those who hunger and thirst for righteousness, for they shall *indeed, really and truly, no-buts-about-it* be satisfied" (v. 6). There it is.

CONCLUSION

It is time for the Christian church to recover the genius of the Beatitudes. They give us the manifesto on Christian life in a non-Christian world that so many people have been desperately searching for. It was right in front of us all along, and it starts with the promise and guarantee of God's blessing. From that starting point, we as individuals, and especially as a church community,

---

11. R. V. G. Tasker, *The Gospel According to St. Matthew: An Introduction and Commentary* (Eerdmans, 1961), 61, quoted in John R. W. Stott, *Christian Counter-Culture: The Message of the Sermon on the Mount*, The Bible Speaks Today (InterVarsity Press, 1978), 35.

are able to live out in a meaningful way the sort of character pictured for us.

Is this your starting point? It makes all the difference to know that you have God's approval, his favor, his blessing. To start with the knowledge that all God's kingdom blessings are ours in Christ means we don't need to fly in fear from the kingdom of man when it turns its aim on us. We are untouchable. It also means we don't need to fight ferociously to win a kingdom. It's not one we earn, anyway; it's one that is bestowed upon us (see Luke 22:29). God builds his kingdom, then he gives it to us. We do not need to drive the world to its knees in submission to us or win victory for Christ though our persuasion and protest. We are already more than conquerors in and through him (see Rom. 8:37).

Some will think I am suggesting that this means we do nothing in this life, nothing to influence the culture, nothing to promote or protect the church. Holiness is far from nothing. It's a sad day when Christians think that living like Christ in the world is not enough for the world. Even the traits set forth in the Beatitudes indicate that there is activity on our part, not mere passivity. How can we make peace without confrontation and rebuke, without bold truth-telling? How would persecution come unless we stand up and speak out? I am in no way suggesting that the culture does not need to be changed; I am suggesting that the first step to change the culture is for me to change. That change is hard, and counterintuitive, but faithful Christians embrace it. Confident of the Spirit's help, we set out together in pursuit of paradox.

FOR FURTHER REFLECTION

1. What is your perception of the "good life"? In what ways does it clash with what Jesus presents in the Beatitudes? How does it conform?
2. Of the three common cultural responses mentioned in this chapter—run, blend, or fight—which are you most tempted toward when facing a hostile or confusing culture? Why do you think that is?
3. Why is it significant that Jesus begins the Sermon on the Mount not with commands but with blessings? What does this reveal about God's priorities for his people?
4. Why is it crucial that we see the Beatitudes not just as virtues to strive for but as qualities formed in us through our union with Christ?
5. In what ways is Jesus the ultimate paradoxical King? How should that shape our own expectations of kingdom life?

1

I MUST DECREASE

> Blessed are the poor in spirit, for theirs
> is the kingdom of heaven.
>
> **MATTHEW 5:3**
>
> *Christ refuses none for weakness, that none
> should be discouraged, but accepts none for
> greatness, that none should be lifted up with
> that which is of so little reckoning with God.*
>
> **RICHARD SIBBES**

HAVE YOU CHECKED your bank account lately? How did you feel about the number in there? My guess is that, even if you are living comfortably, you would feel better if there were more money, not less. Though we may not be multibillionaires, we well know why John D. Rockefeller—the oil magnate and the world's first billionaire—answered the question "How much is enough?" with the line "*Just a little more*."

More is better—right? In our consumeristic age, we are indoctrinated to believe that more stuff solves the problems of life. But the Scriptures teach a different doctrine—a better and truer, though harder, doctrine: *Less* is more. This is a truth that should be applied not to your savings account but to something far more significant: your spirit. That is, your very own self. To be great before God is to be small. We grow up in Christ by growing down in humility. God exalts the humble but lays low the proud (see Matt. 23:12).

This is the lesson behind the first beatitude: "Blessed are the poor in spirit." Familiar words, but do we understand their meaning?

POOR IN SPIRIT

The first thing to underscore is the kind of poverty that Jesus is talking about here. This is not a claim that a crummy financial situation gets us a free pass into glory. There has been some confusion on this point in the church, perhaps enhanced by Luke's parallel passage to the Beatitudes, in which Jesus is recorded as simply saying, "Blessed are you who are poor," with no mention of "in spirit" (Luke 6:20). Additionally, who can forget Jesus's answer to the rich young man's burning question? When the man asked, "What must I do to inherit eternal life?" our Lord replied, "Sell all that you have and give to the poor" (Mark 10:17, 21)! Franciscan monks represent one take on these teachings, as they must "renounce the right to use and dispose of material goods without the permission of their Ministers and Guardians; indeed, after solemn profession they also renounce the right of ownership."[1]

Though God is undoubtedly concerned for the poor and suffering in this life (see Deut. 15:7–8; Prov. 22:22–23), salvation is by grace alone (see Eph. 2:5). Being rich doesn't keep you out of heaven, nor does being poor get you in. It should be noted that it was the rich young man's idolatry, not his wealth, that barred him from the kingdom. Jesus's command revealed that reality: He was exposing the love of this man's heart, and it was not for the Lord. Likewise, the absence of "in spirit" from Luke's account does not alter the meaning. There are other places in Luke where "the poor" stand in as a class of *spiritual* persons, like when Jesus declares his redemptive mission (quoting from Isaiah 61): "The Spirit of the Lord is upon me, because he has anointed me to proclaim good news to the poor" (Luke 4:18). When the biblical data are taken together, it is clear that financial or material poverty is not commended as an inherent spiritual good, much less a necessity to receive God's blessings.

We also need to be careful as to what we mean by *in spirit*. It is not a synonym for demeanor or attitude. Some read this as an

---

1. General Curia of the Order of Friars Minor, *The General Constitutions, the General Statutes of the Order of Friars Minor* (Rome, 2021), 14, available online at https://ofm.org/uploads/The%20General%20Constitutions%20and%20Statutes%20ENG.pdf.

exhortation to live a quiet, diffident, timid existence. Gentleness and meekness are Christian virtues, to be sure, but they are not antithetical to boldness, courage, or extroversion. There will be plenty of mild, unassuming people in hell.

So then, what *does* it mean to be poor in spirit? It's critical that we understand this properly, because the poverty described here is a poverty without which you cannot enter heaven. What Jesus is calling us to is an acknowledgment that, with respect to the merit needed to be saved, we are found wanting—not just wanting but completely devoid of any good! To be poor in spirit is to recognize that there is nothing we have in and of ourselves on which we can bank our eternity. The poor in spirit know that they are empty, and they also know that only God can fill them. And this he promises to do: "For thus says the One who is high and lifted up, who inhabits eternity, whose name is Holy: 'I dwell in the high and holy place, and also with him who is of a contrite and lowly spirit, to revive the spirit of the lowly, and to revive the heart of the contrite'" (Isa. 57:15). What this beatitude is all about, in a word, is humility.

PURSUING POVERTY

So, how can we cultivate this sort of poverty of spirit in our lives? How can we ensure that we are not mastered by the pride that so easily blinds us to our true condition? It should be noted that such an endeavor is particularly difficult in a day and age marked by autonomy and expressive individualism. The slogans of today are "you do you" and "follow your heart." Young people are encouraged to be whomever they want to be. These are the messages in our movies, the themes in our music. They even show up in official legal opinions, such as former Supreme Court Justice Anthony Kennedy's famous remark: "At the heart of liberty is the right to define one's own concept of existence, of meaning, of the universe, and of the mystery of human life."[2]

It is extremely difficult to have a humble view of yourself when the world is preaching to you that your self is actually the most important thing there is.[3] Every beatitude is countercultural, but this one is perhaps more so than the others. And even apart from the cultural pressures surrounding us, the pull of our own prideful hearts is eager to believe that we are the greatest thing there is. But you can't believe that and be poor in spirit. The Christian, therefore, must keep the following three things ever in view if he or she would be poor in spirit and receive the kingdom of heaven.

An Honest Assessment of Our Creatureliness

An honest assessment of our creatureliness starts by acknowledging that God is God and we are not. "I am the LORD, and there is no other," we read in Isaiah. "Besides me there is no God" (Isa. 45:5). The one who is poor in spirit will amen that truth, not rebel against it. Of course, we all have the same impulse as our first parents: to be like God (we also share the folly to think such a goal is attainable!). Instead, we need to think big thoughts about God. We need to put ourselves and God into proper focus: We are small, weak,

---

2. *Planned Parenthood of Southeastern Pa. v. Casey*, 505 U.S. 833 (1992), Justia, https://supreme.justia.com/cases/federal/us/505/833/#:~:text=The%20Act%20requires%20that%20a,before%20the%20abortion%20is%20performed.

3. Matthew Roberts assesses the situation and its theological implications well, writing, "What the Self chooses is right by definition, for the Self is god. What is more, the desires that underly those choices are not subject to any external moral norms but have become the moral norm: they are aspects of the divine will which must be obeyed. Freedom, autonomy, the self, and the self's desires form a nexus which functions in Western thought as a kind of modern pantheon, the thing which is worshiped with the love and willing service due to God alone." Matthew P. W. Roberts, *Pride: Identity and the Worship of the Self* (Christian Focus, 2023), 42.

and finite; he "inhabits eternity" (Isa. 57:15). Well did Solomon cry out, "Behold, heaven and the highest heaven cannot contain you" (1 Kings 8:27). Because he is immense and incomprehensible, even the best thoughts we have of God will never capture him well enough. As the great Puritan theologian Stephen Charnock once put it, "We cannot speak or think worthily enough of him, who is greater than our words, vaster than our understandings."[4]

If you want to work on growing downward in your view of self and magnifying your view of God, try going outside on a clear night. My in-laws live in Arizona, and there's nothing quite like the desert sky on a clear, crisp night. When I look up into our galaxy, with its billions of stars and seemingly endless openness, my chest tightens. It's a strange sensation, one that I can most closely associate with fear or anxiety. But what am I afraid of? That gravity will give up and I will suddenly get sucked into the great unknown? It was only in recent years that I realized the feeling wasn't fear, per se, but *awe*—and indeed, these are closely related! Looking up at the stars gives us an unmistakable dose of reality that we too often ignore: This world is so much bigger than us. In fact, it's greater than we could ever know, and this points to a Creator. The world he has made is truly awful (that is, full of awe).

Do you recall the psalmist's response when he gazed on one of those clear nights like the kind I enjoy in Scottsdale?

> When I look at your heavens, the work of your fingers,
>   the moon and the stars, which you have set in place,
> what is man that you are mindful of him,
>   and the son of man that you care for him? (Ps. 8:3–4)

---

4. Stephen Charnock, *The Existence and Attributes of God*, ed. Mark Jones (Crossway, 2022), 1:292.

Make no mistake about it: Only the poor in spirit ask a question like that.

A Heartfelt Admission of Our Condition

So, God is God, and I am man. That's key. But next I must recognize that I'm not even the man God has called me to be. Indeed, none of us is. We are called to obedience, righteousness, and holiness, but "all have sinned and fall short of the glory of God" (Rom. 3:23). The poor in spirit acknowledge they have no spiritual good to offer the Lord that would earn them a right standing in his holy presence. This is no small problem. Sin affects every aspect of our being: our intellect, our desires, our will. There is no part of our existence that is not tainted in one way or another by sin, rendering us incapable of performing the necessary spiritual good that God requires of us all. The Canons of Dort provide a sobering summary of the effects of our sinful estate. Through sin, man has "brought upon himself blindness, terrible darkness, futility, and distortion of just judgment in his mind; perversity, defiances, and hardness in his heart and will; and finally impurity in all his emotions. . . . Therefore, all people are conceived in sin and are born children of wrath, unfit for any saving good, inclined to evil, dead in their sins, and slaves to sin; without the grace of the regenerating Holy Spirit they are neither willing nor able to return to God, to reform their distorted nature, or even to dispose themselves to such reform."[5]

Since "all people are . . . inclined to evil," it is no surprise that the world is a wicked place. There are countless hardships we endure because our home is broken and people are cruel. In the Old Testament, the term *poor* is often used to describe the person

---

5. Canons of Dort 3/4.1, 3.

who realizes these troubles and calls out to God for help.[6] Consider these examples from the Psalms:

> This poor man cried, and the LORD heard him
> and saved him out of all his troubles. (Ps. 34:6)

> As for me, I am poor and needy,
> but the Lord takes thought for me.
> You are my help and my deliverer;
> do not delay, O my God! (Ps. 40:17; see also Ps. 70:5)

> He raises the poor from the dust
> and lifts the needy from the ash heap. (Ps. 113:7)

While the poor in spirit are sensitive to the realities of sin in this world, they are also willing to make this admission: "Of all the problems I face in life, the greatest problem is *me*." Have you come to that realization? Our greatest problem in life isn't how people treat us, the trials we go through, or the suffering we might endure. Our greatest problem is our sin. "Sin is worse than affliction, than death, than devil, than hell," wrote Puritan Ralph Venning.[7] That's because sin is what keeps us from God—and *our* sin, not anyone else's. Therefore, the poor in spirit cry out to God for deliverance *from themselves* (see Psalm 51:1–3)! The poor in spirit echo the publican: "But the tax collector, standing far off, would not even lift up his eyes to heaven, but beat his breast, saying, 'God, be merciful to me, a sinner!'" (Luke 18:13). The poor in spirit can honestly say, with Paul, that they are the chief of sinners (see 1 Tim. 1:15).

---

6. Sinclair B. Ferguson, *The Sermon on the Mount: Kingdom Life in a Fallen World* (Banner of Truth, 2009), 15.

7. Ralph Venning, *The Sinfulness of Sin* (1669; repr., Banner of Truth, 2021), 201.

Some reading this will feel the weight of that statement acutely. But it must be stated at this point that there is immense comfort when this beatitude is understood. To be poor in spirit is to have the kingdom of God. Both clauses must be equally accepted. We cannot only bemoan who we are by nature and not rejoice in that which we are given by grace. Though we sin much, and perhaps suffer often, Jesus lifts our heads with this word: "Fear not, little flock, for it is your Father's good pleasure to give you the kingdom" (Luke 12:32). How could that not lighten our load and brighten our eyes with joy?

Though the kingdom's blessings will not be fully realized until eternity, there is an immediacy to what this beatitude is promising: "Theirs *is* the kingdom of God—right now!" Dear reader: If you feel burdened by your sin and overcome by your unworthiness, know that Christ has given you himself, and all of heaven is not so lovely and valuable as he is. Here's a paradox to ponder for eternity: The poor in spirit actually possess the greatest treasure. How the humble are lifted high by this reality! It's true that some of us need to hear Jesus's warning to the church of Laodicea: "For you say, 'I am rich, I have prospered, and I need nothing,' not realizing that you are wretched, pitiable, poor, blind, and naked" (Rev. 3:17). But perhaps what you really need to hear is something of the inverse: "You say you are wretched and poor, not realizing that, in me, you are rich and need nothing."

A High Adoration of Our Christ

That is why, to capture real gospel humility, we need to do more than have a low view of ourselves. In fact, to have only a low view of ourselves and our sin and not wed it to a high view of God and his grace is a sign of spiritual pride, not spiritual poverty. As

Tim Keller has said, true gospel humility is not thinking less of ourselves but thinking of ourselves less.[8]

The way to do that is to occupy our thoughts with Another. Yes, we must see our sin, but then we must see our Savior.[9] He is sufficient—indeed, *more than* sufficient—to pay for all our sins. To be poor in spirit is to find our wealth and worth in the righteousness of Jesus Christ. As Paul says, "Indeed, I count everything as loss because of the surpassing worth of knowing Christ Jesus my Lord" (Phil. 3:8). That's because there is nothing greater in all the world than to know Christ and to be "found in him, not having a righteousness of my own that comes from the law, but that which comes through faith in Christ, the righteousness from God that depends on faith" (v. 9).

So, what do you think of Jesus? Who is he to you? Is he still something of a character in a novel—compelling but not quite *real*? Is he an interest to you, or a passion? Do you see him as what Paul calls the "all in all" (Eph. 1:23)? Is your heart bursting with good thoughts and high praise of Christ?

Those who are poor in spirit will always have a ready word to speak about their Savior. He is great not only in the generalities but in the particulars: Jesus is my help for today, my peace in the storm, my joy amid the current trial. Jesus is the Shepherd who brings me back, the Surety who paid my debt, the Mediator who reconciled me to God. He is my Teacher by his Word and Spirit. He is my Friend. He is my Lord. He is my Life. He is the great

---

8. Timothy Keller, *The Freedom of Self-Forgetfulness: The Path to True Christian Joy* (10Publishing, 2012), 32.

9. "It is not the sight of our sinful heart that humbles us; it is a sight of Jesus Christ. I am undone because mine eyes have seen the king." Andrew Bonar, *The Smile of Thy Love* (Christian Heritage, 2024), 31.

Prophet, Priest, and King. He is the fairest of ten thousands, the lover of my soul. Jesus is the Lamb of God, who takes away my sin. My elder Brother who shares his inheritance with me. The poor in spirit are never bankrupt of blessings to bestow on their Savior.

Having Christ, then, rescues the poor in spirit from the incessant pursuit for *more* that motivates the majority of our society. The implied messaging in most advertising is that we are not happy because we are missing something. But you see, to think that our happiness is intrinsically linked to something quantifiable is actually a sad way to live. The poor in spirit will be spared from the consumeristic impulse that says the solution to our trouble is more stuff. The solution is Jesus—*and the poor in spirit have him.* Though the Rockefellers of the world will be telling us we don't have enough, the poor in spirit say, "Thou, O Christ, art all I want, more than all in thee I find!"[10]

START HERE; STAY HERE

It is no accident at all that this beatitude is the first beatitude. It's the threshold that we must cross over to enter into all the blessings that the Lord is eager to give us. Thomas Watson writes, "Why does Christ here begin with poverty of spirit? Why is this put in the forefront? I answer, Christ does it to show that poverty of spirit is the very basis and foundation of all the other graces that follow. You may as well expect fruit to grow without a root, as the other graces without this."[11]

Can we prove that to be the case? I think so. Until we are poor in spirit, we will never mourn (the second beatitude). After all,

---

10. Charles Wesley, "Jesus, Lover of My Soul," 1740.
11. Thomas Watson, *The Beatitudes: An Exposition of Matthew 5:1–10* (Banner of Truth, 1980), 42.

what need is there for it? We are always cheered and comforted by the sense of our accomplishments and ability. Until we are poor in spirit, we are proud and arrogant—and therefore unable to know meekness (the third beatitude). Until we are poor in spirit, we will never hunger or thirst after righteousness. Why would we? We don't see or sense our lack (the fourth beatitude)! We could go on, but it's evident that "Christ begins with poverty of spirit because this ushers in all the rest."[12]

Poverty of spirit does not simply stand at the front of the list in a logical sense; it is the foundational beatitude because, without it, there can be no salvation. It is that significant. To put it quite bluntly, dear reader: You *must* be poor in spirit. Until you are poor in spirit, you cannot enter heaven: "Theirs is the kingdom of heaven." Until I am empty of myself, I can never be filled with Christ. Until I let go of the idols of this world, I cannot receive the kingdom that God desires to give me.

So, this sense of neediness is what starts the Christian life. But it needs to stay with the Christian too—we never outgrow our need for grace. When we think of the debts we have, our impulse is to see them eliminated, and that's good! We want to be out of debt so that we can be richer. But our debt to God is the opposite. The longer we walk with the Lord, the greater our sense of our debt should grow. We must become poorer every day.

CONCLUSION

Does that scare you? Friend, you have nothing to fear by being indebted to a God who is "*rich* in mercy" (Eph. 2:4). If you'll let him, he is ready to pour out his lavish grace on you. To

---

12. Watson, 42.

be poor in spirit is to be rich in grace. To be empty of yourself is to be full of Christ. To be full of Christ is to be the richest one could ever be. What have you to lose by declaring your spiritual bankruptcy to Jesus? He left his home in heaven to purchase your permanent place there. He wore a crown of thorns to ensure that you will wear a crown of glory. He was cursed by God so that, in him, you will be blessed with every spiritual blessing. "For you know the grace of our Lord Jesus Christ, that though he was rich, yet for your sake he became poor, so that you by his poverty might become rich" (2 Cor. 8:9).

FOR FURTHER REFLECTION

1. Why is it important that poverty of spirit is the first beatitude?
2. In what ways does our culture's message of self-sufficiency directly contradict Jesus's call to be "poor in spirit"? How have you seen this tension play out in everyday life?
3. Why is spiritual pride often harder to detect than other sins? What are subtle signs that we might be relying on our own righteousness instead of Christ's?
4. Jesus says the kingdom of heaven belongs to the poor in spirit. What comfort can be found in this message?
5. The world says you must climb upward to gain status; Jesus says you must grow downward in humility to gain the kingdom. In what areas of life do you most need this downward growth?

2

WEEPING MAY TARRY FOR THE NIGHT

Blessed are those who mourn, for they shall be comforted.

MATTHEW 5:4

There is no comfort or joy that can compare with what God gives to those who mourn.

D. A. CARSON

THE GLOBAL MARKET for media and entertainment is north of two and a half trillion dollars, and it's only continuing to climb. Much of that revenue (660 billion dollars' worth) comes from the United States. Netflix, Hulu, Amazon Prime—for many people, these have become something closer to necessities than niceties. Add to that trips to the theater to see the latest Marvel movie, or a vacation to Disney World with the family, and it's evident that—particularly in the West—we live in a world that thrives off of distraction, entertainment, and escapism. Rather than grappling with the hardships of life, many people give their money (and a lot of it) to avoid feeling altogether. We are, as Neil Postman warned, "amusing ourselves to death." In contrast to this, there is a common perception that Christians are a dour lot, unwilling to break a smile or have a good time. One thinks of H. L. Mencken's famous quip that "puritanism is the haunting fear that someone, somewhere, may be happy."[1] Perhaps a beatitude like this one would seem to underscore that perception: *Blessed are those who mourn*. Do we make a virtue out of being gloomy?

Hardly! There is nothing inherently virtuous in sorrow. The first beatitude was not a blessing on any who find themselves in financial straits, nor is this beatitude a blessing on any who happen to be crying. We can often mourn over petty things, even sinful things (like when King Ahab pouted that he didn't have Naboth's vineyard—see 1 Kings 21). We are not to pursue sorrow for sorrow's sake,

---

1. H. L. Mencken, *A Mencken Chrestomathy* (1949; repr., Alfred A. Knopf, 1978), 624, quoted in Leland Ryken, *Worldly Saints: The Puritans as They Really Were* (Zondervan, 1986), 1.

something that is even explicitly condemned by Christ later on in the Sermon on the Mount (see Matt. 6:16). What is actually happening in this beatitude is the confirmation of a special blessing upon a certain type of mourning, one that we can call *spiritual* mourning. Spiritual mourning grieves over sin in the world because it distances us and others from God's good presence. Spiritual mourning grieves over suffering in the world because it witnesses to the fallen nature of God's good creation. But Jesus here promises that if we are sad for the right reasons, we will be made glad in inconceivable ways. The surprise of this beatitude, therefore, is not that it promotes mourning but that it tells us it is safe to be sad. We do not need to numb ourselves to sorrow, nor do we need to be happy as the world defines happiness. Rather, if we embrace godly grief, it will come with godly comfort. This is the sort of gospel paradox we should come to expect in Jesus's discourse on his upside-down, inside-out kingdom. This is precisely the kind of character we should look for in people who are in this world but not of it.

THE UNEXPECTED BLESSINGS OF SPIRITUAL MOURNING

This beatitude, along with other passages in Scripture, teaches us that Christian tears are infused with God's grace. What I mean by this is that God's promise of comfort and blessing applies not only *after* the weeping but even *in* the weeping. As we weep, some wonderful things take place by a work of God. Let's consider some now by asking, How is our spiritual mourning actually a blessing?

Spiritual Mourning Draws Us Away from Sin

First, spiritual mourning is sorrow over our sin. It gives us the proper perspective on sin: something that is grievous to God and that therefore should be grievous to us as well. Though we live in a world that by and large celebrates sin, the church is called to do something different. However, the very fact that so many churches have ceased to condemn sin and now champion it in the lives of their congregants is a sign that we need the Lord to work this sort of spiritual sensitivity into our hearts, for it is anything but natural. To mourn over sin is a sign of God's grace in the heart of the sinner, showing him or her that sin is not to be cherished but to be despised and hated. The salt in our tears is a taste of the bitterness of sin, and "till sin be bitter, Christ will not be sweet."[2]

This beatitude, therefore, builds off the first one. Spiritual poverty calls us to *acknowledge* our sinfulness, while spiritual mourning calls us to *abhor* it. John Stott says, "Confession is one thing, contrition is another."[3] This sort of emotional reckoning with sin requires us to get into the nitty-gritty of our spiritual lives, and that can sound scary. There is an emotional safety, a sort of at-arms-length protection, if I see myself as a sinner in general terms and nothing else. But spiritual mourning requires that I do more. It requires that I consider how I am arrogant, proud, self-centered, lustful, and inconsiderate. Spiritual mourning means I need to acknowledge how I treated my kids last night at the dinner table, or the way I spoke to my wife on the phone, or the wandering thoughts I had during church, or the burning jealousy I have toward my neighbor. The Westminster Divines wisely counseled that "men ought not to content themselves with a general repentance, but it is every man's duty to endeavor to repent

---

2. Thomas Watson, *The Doctrine of Repentance* (1668; repr., Banner of Truth, 1994), 63.

3. John R. W. Stott, *Christian Counter-Culture: The Message of the Sermon on the Mount*, The Bible Speaks Today (InterVarsity Press, 1978), 41.

of his particular sins, particularly."[4] But dare we make ourselves vulnerable in this way? Do not fear: If we own and mourn our sin, Jesus here promises blessing, not banishment. He stands ready to forgive us all our sins and to restore us to the joy of his salvation (see Ps. 51:10–12).

Spiritual Mourning Leads Us to Salvation

This brings us to a second consideration: Spiritual mourning is a grace from God because it leads us to salvation. God doesn't send tears for us to wallow and waste away in them. For the Christian, they become something like a stream whose current leads us to salvation and glory. As Paul writes, "For godly grief produces a repentance that leads to salvation without regret" (2 Cor. 7:10).

We might better appreciate the serious necessity of spiritual mourning if we consider its opposite: hardness of heart, which is equivalent to unbelief (see Heb. 3:7–8, 12). If we will not grieve sin, we will not gain salvation; we will be calloused and immune to God's offer of grace. The great nineteenth-century poet Christina Rossetti captured the need to have a heart that melts and mourns over sin in her poem "Good Friday":

> Am I a stone, and not a sheep,
> That I can stand, O Christ, beneath Thy cross,
> To number drop by drop Thy blood's slow loss,
> And yet not weep?
>
> Not so those women loved
> Who with exceeding grief lamented Thee;
> Not so fallen Peter, weeping bitterly;
> Not so the thief was moved;

---

4. Westminster Confession of Faith, chapter 15.5.

Not so the Sun and Moon
Which hid their faces in a starless sky,
A horror of great darkness at broad noon—
I, only I.

Yet give not o'er,
But seek Thy sheep, true Shepherd of the flock;
Greater than Moses, turn and look once more
And smite a rock.[5]

So we must all pray for this sort of smiting from God. We must pray along with David,

> Search me, O God, and know my heart!
>   Try me and know my thoughts!
> And see if there be any grievous way in me,
>   and lead me in the way everlasting! (Ps. 139:23–24)

We need the conviction of sin that shatters our hearts and melts our eyes to tears. We need to grieve sin in this life, or we will grieve it eternally in the next. It is no wonder, then, that Thomas Watson would say that "tears cannot be put to a better use" than when they are shed over sin.[6]

Spiritual Mourning Brings Us Closer to Jesus

Third, spiritual mourning is a grace from God in that it brings us closer to his Son, not only as the one who saves us from sin but also as the one who weeps with us in our sorrow. Jesus stood at

---

5. Christina Rossetti, "Good Friday," 1866.
6. Thomas Watson, *The Beatitudes: An Exposition of Matthew 5:1–10* (Banner of Truth, 1980), 75.

the tomb of his friend Lazarus and cried. In one sense, he didn't have to do that. As the omniscient Son of God, he knew well that Lazarus would soon be alive (at his own command!). He knew of the resurrection. He knew of the new heavens and the new earth. He knew that this wasn't the end of Lazarus's story. And yet, on the other hand, as the God-man, he *had* to be grieved. Jesus did not come as a stoic solution to the problem of sin and evil. He was not a robot dropped down from glory programmed to save God's people. He was not a cold pharmaceutical for the disease of the human condition. Far from it. He came to "sympathize with our weaknesses" (Heb. 4:15). He saves us from our suffering by suffering for us and with us—and spiritual mourning helps us see that.

Therefore, we cannot grow closer to Christ by stopping our ears or closing our eyes to the sufferings of this life. I once visited someone at a rehab center to have a hard conversation with him about his need to listen to the nurses and actually get out of his bed and exercise. Throughout my visit, the TV stayed on, playing the Game Show Network on a seemingly endless loop, and I struggled to get the patient to pay attention to me. When I asked why he wasn't doing his laps around the hallway, he finally said, "It's too hard, and it hurts too much." Then back to the TV.

It struck me later that this was an all-too-accurate parable of my spiritual life. How often do I respond to the Lord's call of sanctification by turning off my brain and pretending like the sin in my life will just go away on its own? Endless entertainment can't draw us closer to Jesus. Tears can, though. When we weep over the brokenness of the world, the effects of sin, and the suffering of God's people, we experience a deeper fellowship with our Lord and Savior. It is one of the ways we may "share," or "fellowship," in the sufferings of Christ (Phil. 3:10). Truly, as Christians, when we suffer in this life, it is something we do not only *for* Jesus, or *because* of Jesus, but *with* Jesus (see Rom. 8:17). Blessed are those who mourn, for they have a deeper relationship with their Savior, the "man of sorrows" (Isa. 53:3).

Spiritual Mourning Weans Us Off the World

Lastly, tears over sin and suffering make us long for our true home, where God "will wipe away every tear from [our] eyes, and death shall be no more, neither shall there be mourning, nor crying, nor pain anymore, for the former things have passed away" (Rev. 21:4). When I moved away to college, I spent many nights of my first week or two crying myself to sleep. I was terribly homesick. There was nothing wrong with the place I had moved to. The university was great, and the city was exhilarating—but it just wasn't *home*. That pang of sadness was actually a sign of something good in my life: I had a place where I felt safe and loved, and I wanted to be back there. That's how the Christian ought to feel about heaven. Tears are a prayer of sorts, a physical pleading that our Savior would come quickly and take us to where we really belong.

Those who feel entirely at home in this world will not mourn the way that believers do. In fact, the happiest they will ever be is in this life. Just as the sufferings of this life aren't worth comparing to the glory of the next (see Rom. 8:18), the inverse is true for those outside of Christ: The glories of this world are not worth comparing to the suffering of the next. But those who mourn are blessed now because they have the promise of a greater and better future. The Christian's homesickness *will* be healed: "Blessed are those who mourn, *for they shall be comforted*." With what hope the Christian can live life! Even as we hurt, we hope, we trust, we press on, we wait. Anything is worth it if it brings us to the comfort of Christ. As the psalmist puts it,

> Those who sow in tears
>   shall reap with shouts of joy!
> He who goes out weeping,
>   bearing the seed for sowing,
> shall come home with shouts of joy,
>   bringing his sheaves with him. (Ps. 126:5–6)

THE UNMATCHED BENEFITS OF GODLY COMFORT

If Jesus can use our mourning in such blessed ways, what immense blessing ought we to expect from his comfort! If godly grief can bring me to the end of myself, draw me to Christ for salvation, and fix my hope on heaven, then I can scarcely imagine what good things godly comfort can do! Sure enough, the Lord's comfort is not a pat on the back, or a word or two of consolation. It's a transformative and total comfort, reaching into the deepest parts of the human soul and bringing gospel light and joy where all else seems to be darkness and despair.

Godly Comfort Is Transformative

The comfort that God gives to his saints is absolutely transformative. It can take otherwise disheartening and despairing situations and use them as instruments of our consolation. The Thessalonians "received the word in much affliction, with the joy of the Holy Spirit" (1 Thess. 1:6), a paradox that proves the transformative power of God's comfort. The affliction required to receive the Word enhanced the joy. Similarly, Paul describes himself as one who is "sorrowful, yet always rejoicing" (2 Cor. 6:10). Indeed, he and Silas can sit in a prison cell singing hymns of praise to God (see Acts 16:25).

Paul and Silas were not the only ones who could sing in prison. In the mid-twentieth century, Romanian minister Richard Wurmbrand was placed in a prison camp for publicly preaching that Communism and Christianity were incompatible. He writes of his experience, "When I look back on my fourteen years in prison, it was occasionally a very happy time. Other prisoners and even the guards very often wondered at how happy Christians could be under the most terrible circumstances. We could not be prevented from singing, although we were beaten for this. I imagine that nightingales, too, would sing, even if they knew that after finishing they would be killed for it. Christians in prison danced for joy. How could they be so happy under such tragic conditions?"[7] We might wonder the same thing. These Christians are embodying the contradiction of this beatitude: Happy are the unhappy! How can such suffering and sadness be met with such joy? It almost seems supernatural—and that's because it is.

The source of the Christian's comfort is nothing to be found in this world, as it comes from the Holy Spirit himself, who is fittingly called the "Comforter" (John 14:16, 26; 15:26; 16:7 KJV). Through the perplexities of life, the Comforter prays the words we can't (see Rom. 8:26), bestows a peace that the world doesn't offer (see Phil 4:7), and brings into perspective the truth of our suffering: "He shows them that the cross they must bear is so light that it is not worthy of being downcast over."[8] Just as diamonds must be mined beneath metric tons of soil and soot, the Holy Spirit reveals to us the rich blessings that are found even in the depths of suffering.

---

7. Richard Wurmbrand, *Tortured for Christ* (Living Sacrifice Book Company, 1998), 57.

8. Wilhelmus á Brakel, *The Christian's Reasonable Service*, vol. 1, *God, Man, and Christ*, trans. Bartel Elshout, ed. Joel R. Beeke (Reformation Heritage Books, 1999), 186.

Since that is true, what a transformed view of suffering and sorrow you can have in this life! Why should we amuse ourselves to death, and shut out real emotions, when God can use even the hardest things in life in the best of ways? In words often attributed to Puritan Samuel Rutherford, "when cast in the cellars of affliction, remember the great King keeps his wine there."

There is some powerful evangelistic import here. It could very well be that a Christian is never of more use to their unsaved neighbor than when that neighbor is suffering. Why? Because the believer can tell others the great secret of a comfort that transforms even the darkest of situations. While others are "sending thoughts and prayers," we can be sharing Christ and this promise that he gives us in the Sermon on the Mount.

Godly Comfort Is Total

By announcing the comfort of God to those who mourn, Jesus promise to handle every single one of our sorrows. The tears we shed over our own sin and rebellion are wiped away by his pardoning grace: "There is therefore now no condemnation for those who are in Christ Jesus" (Rom. 8:1). That is good news to saddened hearts. Likewise, each and every sigh due to suffering will be answered by our Lord. "You have kept count of my tossings; put my tears in your bottle. Are they not in your book?" (Ps. 56:8). It is as if God is storing up each and every tear that falls from our eyes, a sign of his awareness of them as well as his determination to do something about them. They are in his book, after all. They have made it into a divine to-do list. Though we might not be vindicated from every wrong in this life, the promise is that one day all will be made right. There will be no loose threads. No unanswered troubles. No wounds left unattended. No tears that are not wiped away.

Consider the title Paul gives the Lord at the opening of 2 Corinthians: "Blessed be the God and Father of our Lord Jesus Christ, the Father of mercies and God of all comfort, who comforts us in all our affliction" (1:3–4). Did you catch that? It might be worth reading over again. He is the God not of *little* comfort but of *all* comfort. Not of *some* comfort, but *all* comfort. Not of *much* comfort, but *all* comfort. Not of *most* comfort, but *all* comfort. "All sorts of comforts are stored up in God," says Spurgeon. This means that "no matter what you may require to bear you up under your affliction, God hath just the kind of comfort which you need, and he is ready to bestow it upon you."[9] Even if you should require all the comfort and help and joy that was ever given to all mankind in their affliction, God would have that—and plenty more—to give you.

The comfort that Jesus extends here is not just exhaustive; it's also final. It's a total comfort in that this comfort alone can close the book on earthly suffering. Parents of young children are called to comfort nearly every day. Whether it's scraped knees or hurt feelings, we gather our crying children into our arms and say, "There, there. It'll be okay. Stop your crying. I've got you." And it works! The comfort of a parent is a potent balm for a kid's sadness. But what will happen tomorrow? There will be more tears. More tears will require more comfort. And on and on it will go. But when Jesus says, in the new heavens and the new earth, "Stop your crying," *crying will actually stop*—forever. Can you even believe it? A world without weeping? It is possible, but only through Christ. He who can stop winds and waves can stop weeping too.

9. Charles Haddon Spurgeon, "Comforted and Comforting," *Metropolitan Tabernacle Pulpit*, vol. 45, The Spurgeon Center for Biblical Preaching at Midwestern Seminary, https://www.spurgeon.org/resource-library/sermons/comforted-and-comforting/#flipbook/.

CONCLUSION

This, of course, is a promise for those who belong to his kingdom. Those apart from Christ will dwell eternally in a land of "weeping and gnashing of teeth" (Matt. 8:12). They have their toys and fleeting pleasures to keep them happy now, and sometimes that can entice us. But remember this: Jesus is offering a happiness that lasts forever. Blessed are those who mourn now, for they shall be totally, completely, finally comforted. When tears come (and they will), we do not despair. Our hope was never in a tearless life, but rather in a tearless eternity. So press on, believer: "Weeping may tarry for the night, but joy comes with the morning" (Ps. 30:5).

FOR FURTHER REFLECTION

1. In what ways does this beatitude relate to the first?
2. In what ways does this beatitude bring freedom to a culture obsessed with entertainment and apathy?
3. In what ways does mourning over sin protect us from pride and lead us into a richer understanding of the gospel?
4. Why is it significant that comfort is not merely promised after mourning but often found within it? Have you experienced God's presence even through tears? How might spiritual mourning deepen your intimacy with Christ, the "man of sorrows"?
5. Revelation 21:4 promises a tearless eternity. How does that future hope empower you to embrace and endure tears in the present?

3

THE SURPRISING SECRET TO WORLD DOMINATION

Blessed are the meek, for they shall inherit the earth.
MATTHEW 5:5

Meekness is compatible with great strength.
D. MARTYN LLOYD-JONES

ON THE MORNING of October 7, 2023, waves of Hamas fighters stormed the border of Israel from neighboring Gaza in a bloody surprise attack. The assault was borne out of a religious, political, and geographical dispute that has raged between the two groups for generations. The attack was absolutely horrific. News coverage quickly circulated around the world with the grizzly details: There were beheadings, kidnappings, bombings, rocket attacks, and hundreds killed as militants opened rifle fire on a crowd of unsuspecting concertgoers. One thing obviously absent from Hamas's plan to take back this swath of land they believe is rightfully theirs? Meekness.

Of course, any land grab scheme will wisely exclude meekness from the plans. What a seemingly nonsensical statement Jesus makes here in this beatitude, that the meek will inherit the earth. The meek don't seem to be good for a whole lot, except to be trampled on, ignored, and silenced—certainly not to rule the world. Can you ever imagine turning on the news to this report? "This just in: World domination effected entirely by meekness!"

This is why we need to sit up and listen to what Jesus is saying here. He doesn't often waste his breath on the obvious, but rather loves to speak of the marvelous and mysterious. And this is one of those moments. If Jesus's message were "the strong and powerful will rule the world," we wouldn't need our Bibles. Anyone would deduce as much. But this message of meekness is not natural, and so we need divine revelation and illumination in order to learn it. Could it really be that there is so much more to meekness than the world would have us think? Indeed, could it really be that there is the world to be had for those who are meek?

The power-hungry of society would never believe it. This certainly isn't how our politicians operate, what with their smear campaigns and self-congratulatory stump speeches. If you want to be influential or successful, you need to be loud and assertive. My local gym has a chalkboard in the entrance where the staff write a different "motivation" quote each week. One week I walked in and was greeted with this gem from former US General and Secretary of State Colin Powell: "Have a vision. Be demanding." Anything else puts us in a dangerous place. As John Calvin noted, worldly wisdom tells us "we must hunt with the hounds, because to be a sheep is to risk becoming someone else's dinner."[1]

The church is not immune to this way of thinking, either. In the eleventh through thirteenth centuries, the church was occupied with numerous bloodthirsty crusades to "inherit" the geographical regions of the Bible. Today, the din of warfare has been replaced with the noise of online rants, with many Christians taking to social media to bemoan the sins of the world, lament the obscurity of the church, and call for change. Often the language employed in such rants is as crass as that used by unbelievers. Rallies are held, and PACs are formed—all in an attempt to elevate the church to a place of prominence in society.

Let me be very clear about one thing: Desiring the prosperity of Christ's church is by no means wrong. Far from it (see Ps. 122)! But we must remember that Jesus said *he* will build his church, and he will do so according to his wisdom and methodology, not ours. In the Sermon on the Mount (and the Beatitudes in particular) we find some of the major blueprints for Jesus's building program, and, as counterintuitive as it might seem to us, critical to this project is the meekness of Christ's followers. Meekness

---

1. John Calvin, *Sermons on the Beatitudes* (Banner of Truth, 2006), 34.

is a gift of God's Holy Spirit that he produces in the lives of the born-again and that he uses to advance the cause of his church. The kingdoms of this world *will* become the kingdom of our Lord and of his Christ (see Rev. 11:15)—not through massacre, not through might, but through meekness.

And so we ask, *how* is this possible? How could this actually be the case? How do meek and mild people end up inheriting the world? That's where we are headed in this study, but before we get to the *how* of meekness, we need to address the *what* and the *who* of it.

THE WHAT OF MEEKNESS

This third beatitude rounds out something of an initial triad within the nine. These three all have as their focus the theme of humility.[2] Poverty of spirit is the humble recognition that there is nothing in us that can merit our salvation. Spiritual mourning is the natural response to that humbling recognition. Meekness is the proof of that humility to the rest of the world. It's spiritual humility in its fullest and final form: I am lowly not just in my own eyes or the eyes of God but in the eyes of others, too. Meekness is humility that flows from the heart of an individual to their hands. It produces something discernible to those who are watching. What does it look like, exactly? How does meekness inform our engagement with others? We could highlight three things.

Looking to the Needs of Others

First, the meek individual *looks to the needs of others*. They are not self-obsessed, and they allow no time for self-promotion. The

---

2. See Jonathan T. Pennington, *The Sermon on the Mount and Human Flourishing: A Theological Commentary* (Baker Academic, 2017), 117–18.

late businessman Chuck Feeney is a good example, a man whom one biographer dubbed "The Billionaire Who Wasn't."[3] Though he was one of the richest men who ever lived, Feeney didn't act like it. He never flew first-class, and he stayed in a rented apartment. He gave away billions of dollars to philanthropic causes. Perhaps most impressive is the comment made by *New York Times* columnist Jim Dwyer, who said that not a single one of the *thousands* of buildings across five continents built with Feeney's money bear his name.[4] He was not interested in self-promotion.

Just as importantly, the meek are not interested in self-pity either. Feeling bad for ourselves is every bit as self-focused as feeling good about ourselves. When I sulk that I got passed over for a promotion or wasn't invited to the party with my peers, it could be because I have too high a view of myself. Put another way, God-given meekness helps us remove ourselves from the center of the universe, whether we put ourselves there through self-promotion or self-pity. We see that the world does not revolve around us, and in that we rejoice.

My grandfather was fond of telling one riddle (yes, he only knew the one). It begins with the line "Pretend you are a bus driver." The riddle proceeds to go into cumbersome detail about the bus driver's route—what streets are stopped at, what the weather is like, how many people are picked up, how many are dropped off, and so on. One listens intently to these details, preparing for the question that the riddler will pose, which, after some time, is simply this: "What color are the bus driver's eyes?"

---

3. See Conor O'Clery, *The Billionaire Who Wasn't: How Chuck Feeney Secretly Made and Gave Away a Fortune* (PublicAffairs, 2013).
4. Jim Dwyer, "'James Bond of Philanthropy' Gives Away the Last of His Fortune," *New York Times*, January 5, 2017, https://www.nytimes.com/2017/01/05/nyregion/james-bond-of-philanthropy-gives-away-the-last-of-his-fortune.html.

If executed well, the question seems to come out of nowhere, and most people are stumped. The key is to remember the opening sentence: "Pretend *you* are a bus driver." The riddle works when you forget you're in it and focus instead on all the other details. That's when the Christian life starts to work properly, too. "Do nothing from selfish ambition or conceit, but in humility count others more significant than yourselves" (Phil. 2:3).

You have likely had the experience of someone politely turning down an offer you made with a statement akin to "Don't do that just on my account." A meek response to that is "That's precisely *why* I want to do it." It's not our interests that should be in the driver's seat of our decisions; it's the interests of others. Meekness makes time for people. Meekness makes meals for people. Meekness packs boxes for people. Just about the only time it's wise to help yourself before helping others is when oxygen masks are deployed. But that's the principle the world wants us to live by in all of life. "Self-care isn't selfish." "Choose you." "The most important thing in life is your personal happiness." Once again, the Beatitudes come in to turn things upside down from the way we're used to seeing them. But if we just think about it for a moment, it makes perfect sense: The Bible's call to meekness is actually what gives society its joy. What a miserable existence life would be if we never experienced the selfless care and compassion of others!

Of course, the greatest need of those around us is salvation. Peter calls us to a readiness to share the good news of Christ with our neighbors, and he says that meekness must mark such encounters. We don't berate unbelievers for their lack of faith, nor do we run from opportunities to witness out of a fear of man; rather, we must be "prepared to make a defense to anyone who asks [us] for a reason for the hope that is in [us]; yet do it with *gentleness* and respect" (1 Peter 3:15).

Living with the Weaknesses of Others

Second, the meek individual also *lives with the weaknesses of others*. Oftentimes when the New Testament authors employ the word for meekness (*praus*), they do so to instruct believers in bearing with the sins and shortcomings of others:

> Brothers and sisters, if anyone is caught in any transgression, you who are spiritual should restore him in a spirit of *gentleness*. (Gal. 6:1)

> I therefore, a prisoner for the Lord, urge you to walk in a manner worthy of the calling to which you have been called, with all humility and *gentleness*, with patience, bearing with one another in love. (Eph. 4:1–2)

> Put on then, as God's chosen ones, holy and beloved, compassionate hearts, kindness, humility, *meekness*, and patience, bearing with one another and, if one has a complaint against another, forgiving each other; as the Lord has forgiven you, so you also must forgive. (Col. 3:12–13)

> The Lord's servant must not be quarrelsome but kind to everyone, able to teach, patiently enduring evil, correcting his opponents with *gentleness*. (2 Tim. 2:24–25)

This is a virtue essential for the well-being of the church. Though the church is Christ's kingdom on earth, it is far from perfect. When our Lord brings us into his kingdom, we bring our sins with us—but how we deal with sin is what truly sets us apart from the world. How do the meek live in a society filled with sinners? We recognize that there is no ultimate pleasure or value in retaliation. We don't get a high by putting other people down. We don't discard those who mess up, but rather we believe in second, third, fourth—even seventy-seventh chances (see Matt. 18:21-22)! It is those who are meek who have the Spirit-given impulse to live patiently with the weakness of others. This makes sense—after all, those who are poor in spirit and who mourn their own condition will be the last to cast judgment on others. When the church lives out this beatitude, it proves itself to be a people in pursuit of paradox—finding satisfaction and success not according to common sense but according to God's Word.

Learning from the Wisdom of Others

Finally, the meek individual *learns from the wisdom of others*. Meekness tells me I don't have all the answers and prepares me to receive them from others—and, most importantly, from the Lord himself. Again, we see how this is a distinctly *Christian* virtue. James says, "Therefore put away all filthiness and rampant wickedness and receive with meekness the implanted word, which is able to save your souls" (James 1:21). Without a meek spirit, we would never listen to a thing God had to say! But once we are poor in spirit, once we mourn our condition, we are ready for and receptive to God's instruction.

This means that meekness is more than a natural disposition toward deference and quietness. We all know plenty of people like that: They roll with the punches, they don't draw attention to themselves, and they don't make waves. Is that what Jesus is pronouncing a blessing upon here in Matthew 5? No. With an eye to James 1, we see that this beatitude is about the Spirit-wrought change in our hearts that opens them to the soul-saving Word of God. Those who are meek wait upon and are ready to do God's will, not their own—and there is *always* blessing in that.

THE WHO OF MEEKNESS

Having sketched out a definition of what meekness looks like, we are probably even more puzzled as to how it could possibly lead to the blessing that Jesus promises in the Sermon on the Mount: inheriting the earth. But we should ask ourselves, What happened to the man who exemplified these qualities perfectly? It is not without significance that the one time in all of Scripture that Jesus describes his own character, he uses this idea of meekness: "Take my yoke upon you, and learn from me, for I am gentle [*praus*—the same word translated as "meek" in Matt. 5:5] and lowly in heart, and you will find rest for your souls" (Matt. 11:29).

We cannot properly understand the concept of spiritual meekness unless we look for it in Christ. And when we look to Christ, we see not only one who was meek but also one who has inherited the earth. Paul's grand Christ-hymn of Philippians 2 is our guide:

> Have this mind among yourselves, which is yours in Christ Jesus, who, though he was in the form of God, did not count equality with God a thing to be grasped, but emptied himself, by taking the form of a servant, being born in the likeness of men. And being found in human form, he humbled himself by becoming obedient to the point of death, even death on a cross. Therefore God has highly exalted him and bestowed on him the name that is above every name, so that at the name of Jesus every knee should bow, in heaven and on earth and under the earth, and every tongue confess that Jesus Christ is Lord, to the glory of God the Father. (Phil. 2:5–11)

What do we see here? A mission that is marked by quietness, obscurity, and weakness ends in something entirely different. He who was once despised by the world will be hailed by it: Every tongue confesses his kingship, every knee bows in submission. Jesus knew this was where he was headed as he prayed to the Father before his crucifixion, "Glorify your Son that the Son may glorify you, since you have given him authority over all flesh" (John 17:1–2), or even as he told his disciples before the ascension, "All authority in heaven and on earth has been given to me" (Matt. 28:18).

That's one reason why he didn't fall prey to Satan's tempting offer to give him the kingdoms of the world—he knew that they were already his and that he would enjoy them in God's timing and in God's way. Jesus clearly understood that meekness was in no way an abdication of his authority; rather, it was the God-ordained path to exercising and enjoying it. Now nothing is beyond his rule or reign. As the author of Hebrews says, "Now in putting everything in subjection to [Christ], [God] left nothing outside his control." Of course, this requires faith on our part, since "at present, we do not yet see everything in subjection to him" (Heb. 2:8). But what is now veiled will one day be revealed to the entire watching world, when the humble Son of God returns on a great white warhorse to judge the living and the dead (see Rev. 19:11).

This trajectory in the life of our Savior thus establishes a pattern that Jesus is speaking of in the Beatitudes. More than that, Jesus is simply receiving what God had promised humanity from the very beginning. "The meek shall inherit the earth" is actually where humanity started. From the very earliest days of creation, mankind was privileged to steward and rule over God's world (see Gen. 1:26–28). The only requirement was a meek and humble submission to the Lord. All Adam had to do was obey the simple commands: guard, keep, and do not eat. If he did this, all the world would be his, but in pride he refused, desiring more than what was offered him. Though the nation of Israel was also given a chance to inherit this blessing (see Gen. 17:8), it is not until Christ that we find the perfectly submissive servant of God who receives the reward promised all the way back in the garden.

If we think meekness and world-inheritance are two contradictory concepts, if we're prone to doubt Jesus's pronouncement of blessing on his mild, self-forgetful followers, then we have only to look to his own life for the proof. This is the way God works: "God opposes the proud but gives grace to the humble" (James 4:6; see also Prov. 3:34). That's not an empty platitude; it's proven to be true in the very life of our Savior.

THE HOW OF MEEKNESS

In this, then, is the answer to that question we began with: How is it that the meek can possibly inherit the world? How is that those whom the world tramples over will one day have it all? The answer is found in Christ. Quite literally, *in* Christ—it is our union to the eternal Son of God, the crowned prince of the universe, that ensures our inheritance of it one day. The gospel tells us that, by faith, we will share in all that is rightfully Christ's. We are "fellow heirs with Christ, provided we suffer with him in order that we may also be glorified with him" (Rom. 8:17). So, how does meekness get us such an inheritance? Because it gets us such a Christ.

When Jesus says that the meek will inherit the earth, he is not hinting at some future uprising. It's not as though the meek will inherit the earth because, one day, they will rise up against their enemies, pitchforks and torches in hand, under the rallying cry "We aren't gonna take it anymore!" To do so would be to inherit the earth by abandoning their meekness. But the key here is to understand that meekness is a feature, not a flaw, in Christ's kingdom.

Christians inherit the earth not despite their meekness but because of it. Again, this is the pattern established by Jesus himself. The meekness that took him to the cross and then the tomb is the same meekness that took him to the throne in heaven. Likewise, through our meekness—our willingness to accept the Word of God by faith and rejoice in a servant-Savior who conquers through crucifixion—believers enter into the majesty and reign of him who is the King of Kings and the Lord of Lords (see Rev. 19:16). And what we are inheriting is something so much greater than this fallen earth—something better than the Middle East, something better than the garden of Eden, even. We are receiving a fully renewed, fully restored world—we will reign with Christ over the new heavens and the new earth. That's what meekness gets us! So, here's what we need to remind ourselves: To be meek isn't to accept defeat; it's to receive ultimate and total victory.

What's your response to that reality? How are you going to let that shape your life in the here and now? Paul says this theology should actually help settle Christian disputes:

> When one of you has a grievance against another, does he dare go to law before the unrighteous instead of the saints? Or do you not know that the saints will judge the world? And if the world is to be judged by you, are you incompetent to try trivial cases? (1 Cor. 6:1–2)

Paul is saying, "You will rule the world—can't you figure out how to get along with one another? Why argue over petty things when you have it all?"

This reality should also put into perspective the losses we incur in this life. What is loss, after all, to the one who has "all things" in Christ (1 Cor. 3:21)? In a piece titled "Always Rejoicing," originally published in the *New York Observer* in 1868, one poet captured the idea well: "The peace of Christ makes fresh my heart, a fountain ever springing. All things are mine since I am His—how can I keep from singing?" The meek Christian is the joyful Christian.

The meek Christian is also the confident and calm Christian, the one who stands assured in the grace of God no matter what comes in this life. Do you think the world is changing? Is your impulse to fight to keep things the way they are supposed to be? Some in the church today feel a sense of panic or dread as society continues its push to sideline Christianity. The promise of this beatitude should challenge any instinct to clamor for control. Is your impulse to fear the unknown of tomorrow? Jesus actually quotes from Psalm 37 in this beatitude, which is about a godly response in the face of wickedness:

> For the evildoers shall be cut off,
>   but those who wait for the LORD shall inherit the land.
>
> In just a little while, the wicked will be no more;
>   though you look carefully at his place, he will not be there.
> But the meek shall inherit the land
>   and delight themselves in abundant peace. (Ps. 37:9–11)

The meek do not fight, and they do not fear—they trust in the Lord, for whom all things are possible. They stand confident in the Lord and what he has promised to give them.

CONCLUSION

This understanding will transform the way you live in the world. There is no need to throw elbows and push our way to the top when we're already there. There is no need to seek the approval of the world when we have the approval of God. There is no need to fear loss in this life when gain is promised us in the next. We have no need to posture for power; in Christ we already have it. "If we endure, we will also reign with him," Paul reminds us (2 Tim. 2:12). In other words, we can afford to be demeaned. We can afford to be ignored. We can afford to not get our way. It's no loss to us, since nothing can threaten the unshakable promises of God or the unfading inheritance that is ours in Christ Jesus.

FOR FURTHER REFLECTION

1. How does this beatitude relate to the previous two?
2. Why is it difficult to live with the weaknesses of others, and how can cultivating meekness transform the way we handle relational tension in the church?
3. In a world that prizes self-promotion, assertiveness, and status, how can Christians live out the humility of meekness without appearing passive or disengaged?
4. Self-promotion and self-pity are both forms of spiritual pride. How does meekness help cure both?
5. What does it mean that the meek "shall inherit the earth"? How does this promised future reshape your ambitions and your daily posture toward power, position, and recognition?

4

SATISFACTION GUARANTEED

Blessed are those who hunger and thirst for righteousness, for they shall be satisfied.

MATTHEW 5:6

You have made us for yourself, O Lord, and our hearts are restless until they rest in You.

ST. AUGUSTINE

A SLOGAN FOR a popular American restaurant chain is "Come hungry, leave happy." The catchy phrase expresses what makes any restaurant successful: attracting would-be diners by playing on their growling stomachs with the promise of satisfaction. As the slogan implies, hunger is a sort of unhappiness. We get that. No one needs a dictionary to define the portmanteau *hangry* (why did it take so long for us to come up with that?). Yet in this beatitude, Jesus says there is a sort of hunger that makes one happy (recall that the word for *blessed* in the Greek could also be translated as *happy*). "Happy are the hungry!"—really? Could there be anything more absurd? To speak of hunger and thirst is to speak of want, or lack. It implies the absence of something desired. Why should we be happy if we're missing out on something that we really need? The reason is because of the nature of the hunger that Jesus speaks of, as well as the nature of the filling. If we long for the right things, we will be filled in real and lasting ways.

THE HUNGRY SOUL

Those reading through Matthew's gospel get to this beatitude and will likely think of the previous chapter and Jesus's rejoinder to the devil during his temptation (quoting from Deuteronomy): "Man shall not live by bread alone, but by every word that comes from the mouth of God" (Matt. 4:4). The beatitude pronounces that all will be well for those who have the right sort of hunger, who prioritize the things of God even above physical necessities. Blessed are those who can say, with Jesus, "My food is to do the will of him who sent me and to accomplish his work" (John 4:34). We can explore this further by asking two things: What is Jesus saying about *how* we should hunger? And what is he saying about *what* we should hunger?

How the Hungry Soul Desires

The metaphor of hunger and thirst here is very helpful, for it shows us the seriousness with which we must pursue the things of God. To say that righteousness is something we hunger for is to say that it's something we need. In fact, it's a matter of life and death. The image of hunger and thirst helps us distinguish between wants and needs. My children want to play video games and get upset if I deny them. The stakes would be unthinkably higher if I were to deny them the food they need. The righteousness of God is a matter of need for the Christian. We want it, yes, but we want it because we need it. Consider how the psalmist describes his longing for God in similar language: "O God, you are my God; earnestly I seek you; my soul thirsts for you; my flesh faints for you, as in a dry and weary land where there is no water" (Ps. 63:1).

The desire is serious. It can't be put off. The godly stop at nothing to get more of God in their lives. They will not be contented with vain substitutes; they will earnestly seek after the real thing, and they will not stop until they have acquired it. That means they will want more prayer, more Bible, more preaching, more communion with the saints, more godly conversation, more heavenly meditation. A desire for these things is a desire for the Lord, who uses these very means to draw us into a deeper relationship with himself. This hunger is, therefore, the sign of spiritual life in an individual. Just like a newborn cries for her mother's milk, Christians are to "long for the pure spiritual milk, that by it you may grow up into salvation" (1 Peter 2:2).

To be uninterested in the things of God is a most perilous position. The elderly and the unwell need careful monitoring, since they will often have no appetite and unintentionally starve themselves of needed nutrients because they don't eat. Hunger is a sign of life—dead men don't hunger. Likewise, spiritual hunger is a sign of spiritual life. Martyn Lloyd-Jones presses the seriousness of the issue: "I do not know of a better test that anyone can apply to himself or herself in this whole matter of the Christian profession than a verse like this. If this verse is to you one of the most blessed statements of the whole of Scripture, you can be quite certain you are a Christian; if it is not, then you had better examine the foundations again."[1]

What the Hungry Soul Desires

What is meant by "righteousness" in this verse? There are probably two primary ideas at play here. The first is a personal righteousness. R. T. France explains that when Matthew uses this word in his gospel, he is "overwhelmingly concerned with right conduct, with living the way God requires."[2] R.C. Sproul, similarly, says that "real righteousness is, simply, doing what is right."[3]

The way the Christian receives this sort of personal righteousness is twofold: through the twin benefits of justification and sanctification that come through faith in Jesus Christ. As the Westminster Shorter Catechism explains, "Justification is an act of God's free grace, wherein he pardoneth all our sins, and accepteth us as

---

1. D. Martyn Lloyd-Jones, *Studies in the Sermon on the Mount* (Eerdmans, 1987), 72.
2. R. T. France, *The Gospel of Matthew*, New International Commentary on the New Testament (Eerdmans, 2007), 167.
3. R.C. Sproul, *Matthew*, St. Andrew's Expositional Commentary (Crossway, 2013), 83.

righteous in his sight, only for the righteousness of Christ imputed to us, and received by faith alone."[4] The imputation of Christ's righteousness makes us right in the eyes of God, and therefore we are pardoned of any and all sin. But God doesn't only impute the righteousness of Christ; he also implants the abiding presence of his Holy Spirit. As the Catechism goes on to explain, by the Holy Spirit "we are renewed in the whole man after the image of God, and are enabled more and more to die unto sin, and live unto righteousness."[5] This is what the Christian longs for: less sin, more holiness.

Second, the hungry soul also longs to see righteousness in the world. Jeremiah Burroughs took this to be the primary meaning behind "righteousness" in this beatitude. He writes,

> Christ looks upon His disciples and, as if speaking to them, says, "You are likely to encounter many unrighteous dealings in the world. You will witness the prevailing injustice and unrighteousness. However, it will pain and grieve your souls to observe the unrighteousness in the world. You will long for a time when righteousness will prevail and govern among humanity." Blessed are you! Do not involve yourselves in their unrighteous dealings. Instead, when you witness such injustice in others, let your desires be for the time when righteousness will prevail in the world. Blessed are you for hungering and thirsting in this manner.[6]

A desire to see the world operate righteously is hardwired into all of us because we were made in the image of a God who is

---

4. Westminster Shorter Catechism, answer 33.
5. Westminster Shorter Catechism, answer 35.
6. Jeremiah Burroughs, *Exposition of the Beatitudes: The Saint's Happiness* (London, 1660). Available online at https://www.monergism.com/exposition-beatitudes-ebook.

himself righteousness. You do not need to be a believer to know the difference between good and evil. We have an innate sense that equity and justice are good and that oppression and violence are bad. In 1997, Jewish philosopher Leon Kass set forth the idea of "the wisdom of repugnance," which suggested that an innate negative revulsion to something could be evidence of that thing's inherently evil qualities.[7] I like Kass's more colloquial term for this concept better: *the yuck factor*. There are wicked things in this world to which the only proper response is to sigh, weep, or even gag. The yuck factor can only get you so far, though, because we are also prone to "suppress the truth" in unrighteousness (Rom. 1:18). We can become so desensitized to what is wrong that we can't distinguish it from what is right. By and large, Paul's assessment of the fallen human race is that the yuck factor has failed us. We have fallen so far that "none is righteous"—nor does anyone even desire to be (Rom. 3:10).

THE EMPTY WORLD

At bottom, the desires both to be righteous and to see righteousness flourishing in the world are desires for Christ, "the Righteous One" (Acts 3:14; 7:52). This distinguishes the Christian from the non-Christian. To some degree, all people want to *be* better. While the unbeliever will try countless methods of self-improvement, Christians know the only way to be better is to be made new (see 2 Cor. 5:17). Likewise, even when unbelievers acknowledge the disarray of the world and long for something better, they differ from Christians in *where* they look for satisfaction. The unbeliever who

---

7. See Leon R. Kass, "The Wisdom of Repugnance," *New Republic*, June 2, 1997, 17–26.

is fed up with the world can still only conjure a solution to his or her woes that is found within the world. But the world, even with all its alluring trappings, can't offer real satisfaction—just as there is not a single drop of water in the entire ocean that can save the sailor who is dying of thirst.

One thinks of twenty-seven-year-old Tom Brady, who, in a 2005 interview with *60 Minutes*, asked in total bewilderment and complete honesty, "Why do I have three Super Bowl rings and still think there is something greater out there for me? . . . There's gotta be more than this. I mean . . . this can't be what it's cracked up to be. I mean, I've done it. I'm twenty-seven. . . . What else is there for me?" The interviewer then asks, "What's the answer?" Brady replies, in near despair, "I wish I knew."[8]

C. S. Lewis, if he had been there, would have told him, "If I find myself a desire which no experience in this world can satisfy, the most probable explanation is that I was made for another world."[9] Lewis goes on with remarkable insight:

> If none of my earthly pleasures satisfy it, that does not prove that the universe is a fraud. Probably earthly pleasures were never meant to satisfy it, but only to arouse it, to suggest the real thing. If that is so, I must take care, on the one hand, never to despise, or be unthankful for, these earthly blessings, and on the other, never to mistake them for the something else of which they are only a kind of copy, or echo, or mirage. I must keep alive in myself the desire for my true country, which I shall not find till after death; I must never let it get snowed under or turned

---

8. Steve Kroft, "Tom Brady on Winning: There's 'Got to Be More than This,'" 60 Minutes, January 30, 2019, YouTube video, 1:08, https://www.youtube.com/watch?v=-TA4_fVkv3c.

9. C. S. Lewis, *Mere Christianity* (repr., HarperOne, 2001), 136–37.

aside; I must make it the main object of life to press on to that other country and to help others to do the same.[10]

What can we do to ensure we continue hungering and thirsting for the right things? How can we ensure we are longing for heaven, our true home, and Jesus Christ, our highest good, and not searching for lasting pleasure in a place that is fading away? Here are two helps to avoid filling your soul with a world that is ultimately empty.

Meet with God's People

The first thing is to go to church. This path of paradox is not one Jesus intended us to walk alone. Surround yourself with citizens of another world, "those who are eagerly waiting for [Christ]" (Heb. 9:28). Experience heaven on earth as often as you can until you can get to the real thing. That's what the church affords us: an opportunity to step into the realms of glory, if even for a moment. "But you have come to Mount Zion and to the city of the living God, the heavenly Jerusalem" (Heb. 12:22). The psalmist also acknowledged that it was corporate worship that helped orient him toward hope when he had all but despaired of the vanities of life: "But when I thought how to understand this, it seemed to me a wearisome task, until I went into the sanctuary of God" (Ps. 73:16–17). Worship is like that serene moment on a flight when you have finally made it through the takeoff and have leveled out at thirty thousand feet. Here there are no storms or clouds. All is bright and peaceful. This is the world as God sees it, and he gives us a glimpse of it when we come and worship him. The more we have that, the more we will want it.

---

10. Lewis, 137.

Meditate on God's Place

In a similar vein, think upon the things of heaven and the person of Christ often. Practice the lost spiritual discipline of meditation. Contrary to common secular belief, meditation is not about emptying the mind. It is about filling the mind with biblical material. It "involves personalizing and internalizing a segment of the Word."[11] Unlike prayer, which is an output of our thoughts to the Lord, meditation is a prolonged input of God's thoughts into our hearts and minds. It requires that we think about God's truth long enough to learn it and recognize its relevance for our lives. In other words, it takes memorization and application.

To think about heaven and the things of God will make us desire them more earnestly. When I think about food, you know what happens? I get hungry. If your brain is working right, that's what happens to you as well. When we think about food—or see it or smell it—our brains release the chemical called ghrelin, which then stimulates our appetites. Thinking has turned to longing. If citizens of Christ's kingdom are to have a spiritual hunger, then thinking on the place where we will "hunger no more" will trigger it (Rev. 7:16). Or, put another way, we will never long for heaven in our hearts if we don't think about it in our heads. Why should I expect heavenly things to fill my appetite when I'm not even aware of them? If my head is always in the world and the things of the world, that's where my "gut" will be as well. My instinct will tell me there's something more here for me. But if I retrain my brain to focus on the things of God, my instinct will be to find my hope and help in him.

---

11. R. Kent Hughes, *Disciplines of a Godly Man* (Crossway, 2001), 84.

THE BOUNTIFUL GOD

We have seen thus far that a key to kingdom living is desiring righteousness and recognizing that the world doesn't have it. We must look to the One who promises to give it, which is exactly what Jesus is offering in this beatitude. But how is Jesus able to promise the satisfaction of any and all who desire to be filled? Do you view this statement with slight suspicion? We are used to "satisfaction guarantees" that are anything but. Yet when God promises satisfaction, he actually grants it. Here's how: *He gives us nothing less than himself.* The gospel is that God gives us his very self in the person of his Son. God is not giving us a toy, a check, or even a meal. The gospel tells us that in the person of Jesus Christ, God is giving us himself, in all his indescribable sublimity and inexhaustible sufficiency.

Since God is an infinite being, there is no shortage of life and happiness that he can offer. There is no first come, first served with God. There is no "act fast before it's too late." Not in the sense that he will run out of the righteousness that he promises to bestow. In him is found the "fountain of life," which can never run dry (Ps. 36:9). George Swinnock once wrote that "God is a sphere, whose centre is everywhere, and whose circumference is nowhere."[12] To have access to a God like that is to have access to an infinite resource. We may make unlimited withdrawals from this account, and we will never be denied. Nothing can deplete his treasury. We could ask for a world of righteousness from God, and it would be as though we asked for nothing. "You open your

---

12. George Swinnock, *The Incomparableness of God* (1868; repr., Banner of Truth, 2021), 27.

hand; you satisfy the desire of every living thing" (Ps. 145:16). Such a small act (opening the hand), yet such a massive effect (satisfying every living thing).

Note also in this beatitude that God's boundless supply is matched by his boundless grace. He offers us the infinity of his fullness, and at what does he set the price? Simply our desire. Did you catch that? Jesus here does not say that in order to be filled, we must bring money, merit, good works, or polished prayers. He says we just need to bring an appetite. To receive the thing you *need* most in life, you simply have to *want* it. That's the cost. That's it. Jesus is the one who fulfilled all righteousness so we don't have to (see Matt. 3:15)—we just have to hunger for *his*. "All the fitness he requires is to feel your need of him."[13]

This is the lesson of Psalm 81. In this psalm, the Lord pleads with a rebellious Israel to return to him. We can sense his exasperation with the nation: "Hear, O my people, while I admonish you! O Israel, if you would but listen to me!" (v. 8). If you are a parent, you have probably said something similar to your child: "Just listen!" But amazingly, the reason the Lord longs for Israel to listen isn't so that things will go easier for him—it's so that things will go better for them. He has blessings that he is so eager to bestow. "Open your mouth wide," he tells them, "and I will fill it" (v. 10).

If we feel we are lacking, it's not because God is stingy; it's because, in our disobedience or doubt, we have not opened our mouths wide enough to receive all that he desires to give us. It's not that God doesn't have enough; it's that we desire far too little. So, his plea to errant Israel isn't to sit down and shut up but to come back and open up. This is the heart of our God: He loves to give good things to those who walk uprightly (see Ps. 84:11). We

---

13. Joseph Hart, "Come, Ye Sinners, Poor and Needy," 1759.

don't need God to give more; we need to want more. We need to open our mouths wide, and then we shall be filled. If we would only ask, "Feed me till I want no more," we will be satisfied (see Ps. 22:26; Luke 1:53).[14] There is a sweet complement between God and his children: We have problems; he has resources. We have desires; he has satisfaction. We have needs; he loves to meet them. What a happy thing it is to be hungry when your God is a God who says, "I will satisfy the weary soul, and every languishing soul I will replenish" (Jer. 31:25; see also Ps. 107:9).

CONCLUSION

Mere months before his death, James Montgomery Boice wrote a beautiful hymn that invites us to be filled by Christ. Of all his writings, it was this hymn that became Boice's most beloved in his final days. The reason is clear: When we are closing our eyes on this world, the pleasures of the next become that much sweeter.

> Come to the waters, whoever is thirsty;
> drink from the Fountain that never runs dry.
> Jesus, the Living One, offers you mercy,
> life more abundant in boundless supply.
>
> Come to the River that flows through the city,
> forth from the throne of the Father and Son.
> Jesus, the Savior, says, "Come and drink deeply."
> Drink from the pure, inexhaustible One.
>
> Come to the Savior, the God of salvation.
> God has provided an end to sin's strife.

---

14. Peter Williams, "Guide Me, O Thou Great Jehovah," 1771.

Why will you suffer the law's condemnation?
Take the free gift of the water of life.[15]

Like that hymn, this beatitude is a sweet invitation, isn't it? It's God saying to you, "Come hungry and be happy." When you realize that, what could possibly hold you back?

FOR FURTHER REFLECTION

1. How would you explain to someone what it means to hunger and thirst for righteousness? How is this a hunger that can make us happy?
2. How is it paradoxical that Jesus promises blessing not to those who have righteousness but to those who *long* for it? What does this suggest about grace and sanctification?
3. Does Jesus's idea of deep, soul-level hunger challenge any of your assumptions about fulfillment?
4. Why is it important to see this hunger as both individual and communal? How can the church cultivate a shared hunger for righteousness?
5. How does Christ himself fulfill this beatitude—not only as the Righteous One we long for but also as the Bread and Living Water who alone can satisfy us?

---

15. Excerpt from James Montgomery Boice, "Come to the Waters." Copyright 2000 by Linda M. Boice & Paul S. Jones. Used by permission.

5

DESIRING MERCY

Blessed are the merciful, for they shall receive mercy.

MATTHEW 5:7

True righteousness shows compassion.

MARTIN LUTHER

IN THE PREVIOUS CHAPTER, we concluded with the heart-melting realization that the bountiful and blessed God offers us fullness in him at no cost to us. Grace in Jesus Christ comes to those who simply ask for it, those who want it, those who recognize they need it. We do not need to do anything to earn it. Straight out of the gate, the next beatitude seems to suggest the opposite. It reads, at first blush, as though in order to receive the promised blessing, we need to prove ourselves worthy. It is only the merciful who can ever know God's mercy. Could that possibly be true?

CONDITIONS?

What we find here is something we will encounter again if we continue to study Jesus's teachings. In the famous Lord's Prayer portion of the Sermon on the Mount, we are instructed to pray, "Forgive us our debts, *as we also have forgiven our debtors*" (Matt. 6:12). Likewise, Jesus concludes his teaching on prayer with this difficult saying:

> For if you forgive others their trespasses, your heavenly Father will also forgive you, but if you do not forgive others their trespasses, neither will your Father forgive your trespasses. (Matt. 6:14–15)

Again, this appears to set forth a condition. Is mercy *shown* a condition for mercy *received*? James Boice could not be more emphatic: "Obviously not, unless this statement of Jesus Christ is to be accepted as contradicting all Scripture, including his own clear testimony, or unless we are to abolish the doctrine of grace entirely and with it all hope of salvation. If we are to be dealt with on these terms, no man would ever see heaven. No one would ever receive God's mercy."[1]

Jesus is not teaching that showing mercy to others is a condition for receiving God's mercy. He is saying the opposite: God's mercy to us is the cause of our mercy to others. Or, put another way, when we show mercy to others, we prove that we have indeed received mercy from God. We could think of how Paul puts it in Colossians: "As the Lord has forgiven you, so you also must forgive" (Col. 3:13). God's grace instructs us. The gospel of forgiveness is not only a gift to be received but also a pattern to follow. If we do not follow the pattern, we prove to have never received the gift.

Jesus taught a parable to this effect in Matthew 18. A servant owed an enormous amount of debt to his king. Instead of demanding payment, the king absolved the debt in full. Unbelievably, that very same day, the servant assaulted someone who owed him pennies.

> Then his master summoned him and said to him, "You wicked servant! I forgave you all that debt because you pleaded with me. And should not you have had mercy on your fellow servant, as I had mercy on you?" And in anger his master delivered him to the jailers, until he should pay all his debt. So also my heavenly Father will do to every one of you, if you do not forgive your brother from your heart. (Matt. 18:32–35)

The parable makes the point of this beatitude quite plain. The king's forgiveness was not contingent on the servant's actions.

---

1. James Montgomery Boice, *The Sermon on the Mount* (Zondervan, 1972), 52.

The king acted out of "pity," and there were no strings attached (v. 27). However, the servant's subsequent harassment of someone who was in a similar situation showed the master that he didn't understand the forgiveness he received; rather, he abused it. The indication that we are truly forgiven in Christ will be a changed heart. Mercy shown is proof of mercy received, as well as the confirmation that mercy will be fully experienced in the next life.

DEFINITIONS

But what is mercy exactly? Isn't it often the words we throw around the most in the Christian life that we understand the least? There is no point in continuing to discuss the importance of mercy—whether received or given—without knowing what it is we're talking about. William Hendriksen offers a classic definition when he writes that "mercy is love for those in misery."[2] Likewise, A. W. Pink describes it as "the ready inclination of God to relieve the misery of fallen creatures."[3] "Mercy is kindness exercised towards the miserable," said Charles Hodge, "and includes pity, compassion, forbearance, and gentleness, which the Scriptures so abundantly ascribe to God."[4]

Did you catch the recurring word in each of these definitions? *Misery.* According to the Westminster Shorter Catechism, "the fall brought mankind into an estate of sin and misery."[5] In other words, all those definitions of mercy presuppose sin. That's why Charles Spurgeon would call mercy God's "last-born attribute," as

---

2. William Hendriksen, *The Sermon on the Mount* (Eerdmans, 1934), 54.
3. A. W. Pink, *The Attributes of God* (1930; repr., Baker Books, 1975), 72.
4. Charles Hodge, *Systematic Theology* (1871; repr., Eerdmans, 1981), 1:427.
5. Westminster Shorter Catechism, answer 17.

there was no need for it before sin entered the world.[6] Sin—both our own and that of others—makes us miserable. But God desires to alleviate the suffering caused by sin. And so, as you trace out the biblical story, it becomes immediately evident that the misery of mankind proves to be the theater of God's mercy. It was mercy that stayed the lives of Adam and Eve and clothed them in animal skins when they were naked and afraid. It was mercy that spared Cain's life. It was mercy that heard Abraham's prayer and rescued Lot when Sodom and Gomorrah were destroyed. It was mercy that protected Sarah from a power-hungry and abusive king even when her husband kept silent and did nothing. It was mercy that parted the Red Sea and ended the oppression of God's people. Mercy sent bread to rain down from heaven, and mercy split open the rock and brought forth water, satisfying the hunger and thirst of those wandering in the wilderness. Mercy provided an antidote to the venomous snakebites that afflicted the Israelites. Mercy placed a cruel Sisera in the cunning hands of Jael. Mercy prepared a place for Mephibosheth at King David's table. Mercy winged the ravens to feed Elijah during a famine, and mercy filled a widow's jar with flour enough to feed her family. Mercy brought sight to the blind and strength to the lame. Yes, sin brought misery into this world. But mercy has been outpacing misery ever since.

    The most important thing about tracing out God's mercy is to trace it to *you*. Jesus is telling us that we should see ourselves as the direct recipients of God's mercy. We could not be in his kingdom otherwise. Paul writes,

---

    6. Quoted in Terry L. Johnson, *The Excellencies of God: Exploring and Enjoying His Attributes* (Reformation Heritage Books, 2022), 7. Neither I nor Spurgeon are denying God's eternality or simplicity by employing this term "last-born." Mercy belongs to God's goodness, but it is an aspect of God's goodness that he had no need to display or exercise until sin entered the world.

But God, being rich in mercy, because of the great love with which he loved us, even when we were dead in our trespasses, made us alive together with Christ—by grace you have been saved—and raised us up with him and seated us with him in the heavenly places in Christ Jesus, so that in the coming ages he might show the immeasurable riches of his grace in kindness toward us in Christ Jesus. (Eph. 2:4–7)

He employs similar language when he writes to Titus, "He saved us, not because of works done by us in righteousness, but according to his own mercy" (Titus 3:5). In very personal terms, Paul also recounts his own conversion by appealing to God's merciful character: "Though formerly I was a blasphemer, persecutor, and insolent opponent. But I received mercy because I had acted ignorantly in unbelief" (1 Tim. 1:13). Likewise, Peter can't define the church without talking about God's mercy! "Once you were not a people, but now you are God's people; once you had not received mercy, but now you have received mercy" (1 Peter 2:10).

We need to learn from the likes of Peter and Paul when defining mercy. Sure, it is true enough to say that God's mercy is his loving inclination to help those in misery. But what Jesus is after in the Beatitudes is for us to say, "God's mercy is his loving inclination to help *me*." We must put ourselves in the middle of our definition of mercy. We are and have nothing without God's mercy. We are all sin, but thanks be to God that "there is more mercy in Christ than sin in us."[7] And it's a mercy he is eager and ready to bestow on you. Do you believe that? Do you adore that truth? For the redeemed, for citizens of Christ's kingdom, we recognize that mercy is everything. And therefore we want nothing more than to show it to others.

---

7. Richard Sibbes, *The Bruised Reed* (1630; repr., Banner of Truth, 2008), 13.

BARRIERS

Of course, given the stubborn nature of selfishness and sin, we need frequent reminders and helps to live the way God calls us to. We will have to overcome at least three primary barriers to showing mercy if we are to be faithful followers of Christ. The first is *self-centeredness*, which is marked by an ignorance of other people's needs because we are preoccupied with our own. Sometimes I am so consumed with the issues going on in my own life that I forget other people are suffering as well. A second barrier is *laziness*, or an indifference to people's needs. We might recognize the suffering or struggle of others, but we can't be bothered to do much about it. We think, "Surely if I don't pick up the phone when they call for help, the next person will!" A final barrier is *fear*, which produces a reluctance to show mercy because of what it might cost us. It's one thing to let a friend cry on your shoulder as they tell you about their bad day; it's quite another to hold their hand and walk with them through an entire season of suffering!

Add to these three internal barriers the massive external one: We live in a world that hates mercy. We certainly commend it as a virtue in our film and literature, but on a personal level, things like mercy, compassion, and "letting bygones be bygones" are seen as weaknesses, not strengths. If we forgive, we lose (so we think) power over others, an opportunity down the line to turn a past offense into a future favor. Our world is a cold, cutthroat place—the perfect climate for grudges to fester.

And while it is socially commendable to give to charitable organizations, actually stopping to help a down-and-out individual, looking them in the eye, treating them with dignity—who has the time? Mercy to those who are needy is not natural. I'm not suggesting it never happens—by God's common grace, it does.

But I am saying that to operate under a principle of mercy can feel an awful lot like swimming upstream. Calvin well describes how countercultural this beatitude is: "This paradox, too, contradicts the judgment of men. The world reckons those men to be *happy*, who give themselves no concern about the distresses of others, but consult their own ease. Christ says that those are *happy*, who are not only prepared to endure their own afflictions, but to take a share in the afflictions of others."[8] When it seems like everything is fighting against a merciful lifestyle, what can help us live the life Christ is calling us to? We need motivation.

MOTIVATIONS

As Jesus makes clear in this beatitude, God's mercy will be the greatest motivation for our own. On the one hand, by implication the beatitude reminds us of all that we have *already* received, and thus, from the overflow of a thankful heart, we are willing and eager to reflect God's mercy. On the other hand, by explication this beatitude holds out the guarantee of something that has yet to take place, and so it pushes us on to attain the goal—namely, *more* mercy from God! As D. A. Carson explains, the Christian "is at a midpoint. He is to forgive others because in the past Christ has already forgiven him (cf. Eph. 4:32; Col. 3:13). Simultaneously he recognizes his constant need for more forgiveness, and becomes forgiving as a result of this perspective as well."[9] God's mercy is our motivator!

In fact, elsewhere Scripture informs us that the mercy of God

---

8. John Calvin, *Calvin's Commentaries*, vol. 16, *Harmony of Matthew, Mark, Luke* (Baker Book House, 1981), 263. Emphasis original.

9. D. A. Carson, *Jesus's Sermon on the Mount and His Confrontation with the World: A Study of Matthew 5–10* (Baker Books, 2018), 30.

is to be our primary motivation for *all* we do in the Christian life. In Romans 12:1 Paul writes, "I appeal to you therefore, brothers and sisters, *by the mercies of God*, to present your bodies as a living sacrifice, holy and acceptable to God, which is your spiritual worship." This is the one motivation strong enough to carry us through a life of obedience: God's mercy to us in Christ. When we see Christ hanging on the cross for our sins, no sacrifice we could make will ever seem to be too much. Indeed, we will offer our whole selves as a living sacrifice.

A comprehensive recognition of the mercy we have received is the only thing strong enough to get over those barriers mentioned above. It rescues us from self-centeredness, since it teaches us how undeserving we have been to receive God's love. It pushes us through lazy habits, since God's mercy was active—Jesus came "to seek and to save the lost," after all (Luke 19:10). And it overcomes fear, since God's mercy meets all our needs; therefore, giving of ourselves to help others will never be to our disadvantage, not when our Lord is our Shepherd (see Ps. 23:1). Mercy also motivates us to reach out in love to those who have hurt us and those who are hurting.

Those Who Have Hurt Us

Peter once asked Jesus, "Lord, how often will my brother sin against me, and I forgive him? As many as seven times?" (Matt. 18:21).[10] Is there a limit to the mercy we should extend those who have sinned against us? The rise of so-called "cancel culture" seems to suggest so. "America has forgotten how to forgive," said one journalist when reporting on yet another high-profile individual who

---

10. Some of this material originally appeared in my article "The Fallout from Forgetting Forgiveness," *New Horizons*, May 2022, 8–9, 16.

was canceled for a past sin.[11] Our current culture doesn't know what to do with "the guilty." Beyond losing the *tools* with which to offer forgiveness, I fear we are losing even the *desire* for it. Ours is an inquisitorial age, one that seems to almost relish condemning others.

Sadly, what we see "out there" in the world often reveals the bent of our own hearts. We must be on guard lest we allow the unbiblical, gospel-less standards of the day to infiltrate the church—and where and when they have, we must repent. Timothy Keller wrote, "We who live only by the mercy of God every second of our lives fail to be kind, merciful, generous, gracious, and forgiving every day."[12] Rather than being people of paradox, we are people who just play right along with the rules everyone else is following. May it not be!

Here's what we need to remember: The determining factor in our mercy is not the sin of the offender but the heart of God. Once we plumb the depths of his mercy toward us, once we reach the bottom of that great mine, we can cease to show mercy to others. The only limit to our mercy should be God's love—which is to say there is no limit at all. Christian mercy is meant to be a *reflexive* act. As J. C. Ryle once wrote, "One motive for forgiving others ought to be the recollection that we all need forgiveness at God's hands ourselves . . . day after day we require mercy and pardon. Our neighbors' offences against us are mere trifles, compared with our offences against God."[13]

Mercy is also a *reflective* act. We testify to the character of God when we show mercy even to those who seem to deserve it

---

11. Graeme Wood, "America Has Forgotten How to Forgive," *Atlantic*, March 18, 2021, https://www.theatlantic.com/ideas/archive/2021/03/america-has-lost-ability-forgive/618336/.

12. Timothy Keller, *Forgive: Why Should I and How Can I?* (Viking, 2022), 8.

13. J. C. Ryle, *Matthew: Expository Thoughts on the Gospels* (Banner of Truth, 2012), 185–6.

the least, because that's what God has done for us. In 2015, nine peaceful believers were shot to death by deranged racist Dylann Roof, who had attacked a midweek prayer meeting at Emanuel AME church in Charleston, South Carolina. Only two days later, at Roof's hearing, the victims' families spoke. For a change, the world was watching the church. And what happened? One by one, they each expressed their willingness to forgive Roof, and they called on him to repent and believe. Incredibly, reporter Charles C. W. Cooke for *National Review* tweeted at that moment, "I am a non-Christian, and I must say: This is a remarkable advertisement for Christianity."

Those Who Are Hurting

We can sometimes struggle to extend mercy to those who are suffering. When I lived in downtown Philadelphia, I grew calloused to the extreme poverty that stared me in the face every day I commuted. I rarely went a day without being approached for money. I am not suggesting that showing mercy as Jesus calls us to means always giving money to people who ask for it. I am suggesting, rather, that our inclination should be to help if and whenever we can. Instead, we turn a blind eye to the homeless man at the stoplight; we dismiss the cashier's request to round up to support [insert charity here]. Perhaps we give to an annual drive at a local school or ministry, but what Jesus is after here is "those whose bent is to show mercy, not those who engage in an occasional merciful impulse."[14]

The Bible actually addresses the need to serve the suffering quite a bit. And often when it speaks of the sufferer, it is speaking

---

14. Leon Morris, *The Gospel According to Matthew*, Pillar New Testament Commentary (Eerdmans, 1992), 110.

of us! While we may be in a better financial situation than the panhandler on the street corner, from the Bible's perspective, we are still "poor and needy" (Pss. 40:17; 70:5; 86:1; 109:22). The motivation for showing mercy to the sufferer is the same as that for showing mercy to the sinner: We must see that we are recipients of the very same kind of mercy! We live off of mercy! Do we have a job? That's from God's hand. Do we have a house? That's provided by the Lord. Do we have good health? God has given that to us too. We are debtors to mercy, through and through. "Every good gift and every perfect gift is from above" (James 1:17). Since we are sufferers who have received countless mercies from the Lord, let us refuse to be thankless recipients who never extend that same mercy to others.

Our willingness to show compassion and to reach out toward those in a miserable condition is an indication of our spiritual health. John writes,

> But if anyone has the world's goods and sees his brother in need, yet closes his heart against him, how does God's love abide in him? Little children, let us not love in word or talk but in deed and in truth. (1 John 3:17–18)

Do we have the love of God? Then we shall have the love of neighbor.

That was the concluding point to Jesus's parable of the good Samaritan, a story Jesus tells in response to the question "Who is my neighbor?" Do you recall what made the Samaritan "good," after all? He stopped and helped a sufferer when no one else would. He didn't know anything about the man: Did he deserve what had befallen him? Would he repay him if he were helped? Would he become dependent on the Samaritan's generosity if he dared stop? None of that factored into his decision; he simply helped. And so, Jesus asks his audience, "Which of these three people—the priest, the Levite, or the Samaritan—was a *neighbor* to the beaten-up man on the side of the road?" The answer that a scribe gives is exactly right: "The one who showed him mercy" (Luke 10:37). In other words, mercy is at the very heart of the second greatest commandment: Love your neighbor as yourself (see Matt. 22:39).

CONCLUSION

Does your life reflect the mercy you have received from God? It's something even the best of us need to grow in, undoubtedly. In fact, there is no graduating from the school of God's mercy toward us in Christ. In a cutthroat world that is all "me, me, me," and rarely ever "mercy," cultivate something completely countercultural through deep, prolonged, and regular meditation upon the character of God. It's always appropriate for us to take up Jesus's charge to the Pharisees: "Go and learn what this means: 'I desire mercy, and not sacrifice'" (Matt. 9:13; see also Prov. 21:3). What God wants from you isn't rote, formulaic obedience. He wants not only a life that conforms to the external expectations of his holy law but one that is transformed at the heart by his glorious gospel. Indeed, the gospel is so good that it demands a response—but this beatitude teaches more: The gospel is so powerful that it *creates* a response. Those who have received mercy from God *will* extend it to others, and those who extend it to others have the guarantee of enjoying the immeasurable riches of God's grace on into eternity.

FOR FURTHER REFLECTION

1. How have you seen or experienced the ways in which our culture belittles the virtue of mercy?
2. Jesus says the merciful will receive mercy. Is this a reward for good behavior, or is it something different? How does the gospel help us understand this conditional-sounding promise?
3. How can a church community grow into a people of mercy, rather than one marked by suspicion, judgment, or cancellation?
4. This chapter listed several barriers to extending mercy toward others. Which of those most resonated with you? What other hurdles make acts of mercy especially difficult for you?
5. In what relationships or situations do you need to develop a greater ability and desire to show mercy?

6

DEVOTED TO GOD

Blessed are the pure in heart, for they shall see God.
MATTHEW 5:8

*The clean heart is not the heart pure from sin,
but the heart cleansed and renewed by grace.*
CHARLES BRIDGES

IN THIS SIXTH BEATITUDE, Jesus touches upon a subject that would have been of great interest to the pious Jews of the day: purity. Those steeped in the customs of the old covenant system were well trained to know that purity was critical to a right relationship with God. A major thesis of the entire book of Leviticus, for example, is that defilement, uncleanliness, and impurity only keep you far from God. Those who want to be near God must take purity seriously. Jesus here draws on the teaching and language of Psalm 24: "Who shall ascend the hill of the LORD? And who shall stand in his holy place? He who has clean hands and a pure heart" (vv. 3–4).

But for how seriously the people of Jesus's day took the concept of purity, they were still far from understanding its true meaning. They were often unable to separate the idea from *ritual* cleanliness—that is, the adherence to old covenant stipulations for participating in worship. So, the Pharisees and serious worshipers knew what to eat, when to wash, and who to stay away from so that nothing defiled them and rendered them incapable of entering God's presence with his people. But this was the extent of their concern. In other words, while they might have had the "clean hands" part of Psalm 24 down, they were missing the far more important part: the "pure heart."

So, Jesus draws his listeners, and us, to consider the demands of the Christian life. They are not surface level in the slightest but reach all the way down to the heart. Yet, as we have come to expect, this high calling comes with an even higher blessing. Jesus never requires us to give more to him than he is ready and eager to give to us. Those who take seriously the call to purity of heart will enjoy an unimaginably great reward: beholding the sight of God himself. If that's what's at stake, we'd best lean in and consider this teaching carefully.

THE DEEPEST NEED

External adherence to religious ideals will not cut it in Christ's kingdom. Something deeper than that is required. Jesus is after heart-change here—that is, a total renovation of our intellect, affections, and will—and in the pronouncement of this blessing he anticipates his teaching in later portions of Matthew's gospel. In chapter 15, for instance, the Pharisees accuse Christ's disciples of not following the "tradition of the elders" (v. 2) and maintaining strict standards of ritual purity, like handwashing and eating (or not eating) certain foods. Jesus tells them that, by focusing on the hands, they have missed what matters most—namely, the heart.

> It is not what goes into the mouth that defiles a person, but what comes out of the mouth; this defiles a person. . . . What comes out of the mouth proceeds from the heart, and this defiles a person. For out of the heart come evil thoughts, murder, adultery, sexual immorality, theft, false witness, slander. These are what defile a person. But to eat with unwashed hands does not defile anyone. (vv. 11, 18–20)

A similar denunciation against the Pharisees comes in Matthew 23:25–28:

> Woe to you, scribes and Pharisees, hypocrites! For you clean the outside of the cup and the plate, but inside they are full of greed

and self-indulgence. You blind Pharisee! First clean the inside of the cup and the plate, that the outside also may be clean.

Woe to you, scribes and Pharisees, hypocrites! For you are like whitewashed tombs, which outwardly appear beautiful, but within are full of dead people's bones and all uncleanness. So you also outwardly appear righteous to others, but within you are full of hypocrisy and lawlessness.

Christians are called to care about the thing that no one else can see: our hearts. This beatitude is here to remind us that we can't cut it in Christianity if we think it's like looking over the outside of a rental car. That's the first and last step of renting a vehicle, isn't it? Before you drive away, you need to sign off that there are no scratches or dents (bigger than a golf ball, at least!), and then the attendant has to do the same thing before you can return it. Of course, if the transmission is shot, the alternator on its way out, or the brakes starting to fail, no one would be the wiser, and everyone could go on their merry way. People approach the Christian life in that same kind of superficial way. They take a quick survey of themselves, see if they check off the "good person" boxes, and then never give their relationship to the Lord another thought. That's precisely what Jesus is condemning in the aforementioned passages, and in the sixth beatitude he assures us there is no blessing in it. He does not say, "Blessed are the put-togethers," or "Blessed are the picture-perfects." He goes deeper than all that and says, "Blessed are the pure in heart."

The heart is what matters most. From God's perspective, you could never be a good enough person to make up for a heart that's defiled, corrupt, and impure. It matters too much to be overshadowed by other "advances" or "improvements." If the heart is not saved, nothing is saved. John Flavel, a Puritan pastor, once wrote that "the keeping of the heart is the great work of a Christian, in which the very soul and life of religion consists, and without which all other duties are of no value in the sight of God."[1] The Christian, therefore, strips away any pretense and deals with the heart.

In so many other areas of life, we know to focus on the main thing, to protect what matters most. We just got a new couch, and the first thing our kids got to do was sit on it and listen to us lecture them on all the no-nos. No shoes, no jumping, no climbing, no eating, no drinking. But we have an old couch in the basement that they can essentially do whatever they want on. The problem with the Pharisees—and many people today—is a problem of priority, something akin to zealously protecting the unimportant basement couch while not caring if the brand-new one upstairs stays clean. We must engage our best time and our strongest energies in keeping pure that which is the greatest concern: our hearts.

THE PUREST LOVE

It is quite natural, then, to next ask, What does it mean to keep the heart pure? The pure heart that Jesus is after here is pure in the same way that bottled water companies advertise their product. "Pure spring water" means that the water comes from a single source. There is no mixture, no add-ins, no chemical processes undergone. It's just water. To have a pure heart is to have a heart that comes with no additives, no contaminants. It is made up of one ingredient: devotion to God. In his superb book on the heart, Craig Troxel helpfully explains it like this: "[The pure heart] is not divided in its priorities or confused by mixed motives. It is

---

1. John Flavel, *Keeping the Heart: How to Maintain Your Love for God* (Christian Heritage, 2021), 107.

a heart devoted to God and not distracted by idols, selfishness, pride, fame, or money.... Its thoughts, speech, and behavior are increasingly marked by a singular purpose, as the dross of compromise is being scraped away. Christ is purging the desires so that they focus on their chief end—to glorify God and enjoy him. *Purity of heart is to desire one thing*."[2]

Further clarity comes from James's teaching, when he says that those who need to purify their hearts the most are the "double-minded": "Draw near to God, and he will draw near to you. Cleanse your hands, you sinners, and purify your hearts, you double-minded" (James 4:8). Similarly, Peter and Paul both liken purity to *sincerity* (see Col. 3:22; 1 Tim. 1:5; 1 Peter 1:22), which is the opposite of duplicity. In other words, the pure in heart do not have two ways of operating: one that pleases God, and one that pleases self. They are entirely devoted to pleasing God, and no other. The pure in heart make it their aim to fulfill that greatest of all commandments: to "love the Lord your God with all your heart" (Deut. 6:5; see also Matt. 22:37).

The pure heart is the focused heart. Its aim is the glory of God alone. John Newton, in one of his pastoral letters, writes about this kind of purity. He says to be pure in heart means "that we have but one leading aim, to which it is our deliberate and unreserved desire, that everything else in which we are concerned may be subordinate and subservient. In a word, that we are devoted to the Lord, and have by grace been enabled to choose him, and to yield ourselves to him, so as to place our happiness in his favour, and to make his glory and will the ultimate scope of all our actions. He well deserves this from us."[3] Its affection is enlarged by those things

---

2. A. Craig Troxel, *With All Your Heart: Orienting Your Mind, Desires, and Will Toward Christ* (Crossway, 2020), 98. Emphasis mine.

3. John Newton, "Letter XXIII," in *The Works of John Newton* (1839; repr.,

that are true, good, and beautiful, and nothing that is corrupt or wicked. To be pure in heart is to say with the psalmist, "Whom have I in heaven but you? And there is nothing on earth that I desire besides you" (Ps. 73:25).

Perhaps at this point in your reading you are thinking what I am as I'm writing: *How could I possibly have a heart like this?!* If we return to our bottled water analogy, spring water is *naturally* pure—it comes out of the spring free of contaminants. But it's not the only pure water out there. Other water can be *purified*—through distillation, ozonation, reverse osmosis, and a whole host of other filtration processes, the pollutants can be removed to make the water potable. Our hearts are in that latter category. They are not naturally pure, but they can be *made* pure. We need our hearts to be refined and sin to be removed so that only one thing remains: a love for God.

This is the work of sanctification. And something quickly becomes apparent in the Christian life: Holiness is hard, and it often hurts! The metaphor frequently used in Scripture to describe this process of heart-purification is that of refining in a fire (see, for example, Jer. 9:7; Zech. 13:9; Mal. 3:3; 1 Peter 1:6–7). The heat hurts, but it's a pain that leads to a good and glorious end. The Christian should also take comfort knowing that, while this work of purifying the heart is difficult and strenuous, its success is promised to us in the Scriptures! God tells his people that he is sending them the indwelling Spirit to ensure that purity wins out in the end:

Banner of Truth, 2018), 1:210. Again, I am indebted to Craig Troxel, whose insights on this subject drew my attention to this letter of Newton's. Troxel references it in his article "The Cure for Hypocrisy," *Tabletalk*, March 10, 2021, https://tabletalkmagazine.com/posts/the-cure-for-hypocrisy/.

> I will sprinkle clean water on you, and you shall be clean from all your uncleannesses, and from all your idols I will cleanse you. And I will give you a new heart, and a new spirit I will put within you. And I will remove the heart of stone from your flesh and give you a heart of flesh. And I will put my Spirit within you, and cause you to walk in my statutes and be careful to obey my rules. (Ezek. 36:25-27)

The only way to have a pure, undivided heart is by God's Spirit. And this is the Spirit God promises to give to his people. So pray for God's work to be done! You could even use these words of William Cowper to get you started:

> The dearest idol I have known,
> whate'er that idol be,
> help me to tear it from Thy throne
> and worship only Thee.[4]

Or, even better, these words of David:

> Purge me with hyssop, and I shall be clean;
>   wash me, and I shall be whiter than snow.
> Let me hear joy and gladness;
>   let the bones that you have broken rejoice.
> Hide your face from my sins,
>   and blot out all my iniquities.
> Create in me a clean heart, O God,
>   and renew a right spirit within me. (Ps. 51:7-10)

---

4. William Cowper, "Walking with God," 1772.

Of course, our hearts will never be perfectly pure this side of glory. In fact, the more we work at purifying them, the more their impurity will become apparent to us. But we're not after perfection here; we're after the work of God's grace in renewing us from the inside out. When we come to God in Christ, we can have confidence that he accepts us because of Christ's merits and that he is genuinely pleased with our progress, small though it may be. The Westminster Confession of Faith describes good works like this: "The persons of believers being accepted through Christ, their good works also are accepted in him; not as though they were in this life wholly unblamable and unreprovable in God's sight; but that he, looking upon them in his Son, is pleased to accept and reward that which is sincere [*there's the idea of purity!*], although accompanied with many weaknesses and imperfections."[5]

So, to be pure is not to be perfect; it's to be in Christ and indwelt by his Spirit. Even though none can say, "I have made my heart pure" (Prov. 20:9), many can say, "Jesus has" (see Heb. 10:22). "Myriads can witness to the blood of him, who is the Son of God, cleansing [the heart] from guilt, and to the mightiness of the Creator to renew it unto holiness."[6] This should cause us to flee to the fountain of blood that flows from Christ's heart of love, the fountain that alone makes us pure (see 1 John 1:7; see also 3:3).

THE HAPPIEST SIGHT

I wonder if there could be a greater motivation to a life of purity and holiness than the promise that Jesus extends in this beatitude: "Blessed are the pure in heart, *for they shall see God.*" Do

---

5. Westminster Confession of Faith, chapter 16.6.
6. Charles Bridges, *An Exposition of Proverbs* (1846; repr., Sovereign Grace Book Club, n.d.), 343.

you long to see God? Do you understand why it's so crucial that we do? Ever since the fall, we have been prevented from beholding the glory of the One in whose image we were made. That's not right or healthy for our souls. Distance from God distorts everything in life. And for as much as sin sends us foolishly in the opposite direction, the believer has a new—and truer—impulse: to be near God (see Ps. 73:28). They long to be near him so that they can see him.

Seeing God Now

There's a twofold blessing in this beatitude, because the Christian has a "double vision" of sorts. Those who are pure in heart start to see God right now. This makes good sense if purity means a single-minded devotion. What else do the pure in heart fix their eyes on in this life but God and his glory (see Col. 3:1–4)? As Sinclair Ferguson says, "Being pure in heart means letting nothing stand in the way of our vision of Christ."[7] I once got extremely affordable tickets to a highly anticipated concert. When I arrived at the show, I realized why I was able to save so much money: There was a pole directly blocking my view of the stage. I didn't read the fine print close enough—it was a discounted ticket because of the "obstructed view." The pure in heart do not abide this sort of thing. Whatever blocks their view of God has to go, or they must get around and above it until they enjoy an unhindered vista. "The things of earth will grow strangely dim" for those whose hearts are being weaned off of sin and this world and who are growing in holiness.[8]

Although we cannot literally see the Lord in this life, a sign of heart-purity is delighting in the ways we are privileged to glimpse

---

7. Sinclair B. Ferguson, *The Sermon on the Mount: Kingdom Life in a Fallen World* (Banner of Truth, 2009), 37.
8. Helen Howarth Lemmel, "Turn Your Eyes upon Jesus," 1922.

him now. The "eye" for the Christian in this life is faith. By faith, we see God as he reveals himself in Holy Scripture. We see him in the waters of baptism and in the elements of the Lord's Supper. We see his glory in worship. We see his grace in the communion of saints. If that seems unremarkable to you, just remember that sin clouds our view of Christ. With greater purity comes greater clarity, and these ordinary things will become extraordinary opportunities to behold the Lord. This was the psalmist's experience, as he records in Psalm 73: "Truly God is good to Israel, to those who are pure in heart. But as for me, my feet had almost stumbled, my steps had nearly slipped . . . *until I went into the sanctuary of God*" (vv. 1–2, 17). The psalmist revels in the goodness that God shows to the pure in heart, but he was on the brink of not being one of them. Evil had blocked his view of God, and the way to get it back was to return to his true love through worship in the Lord's sanctuary.

This beatitude invites us to ask a question: *How well do I see Christ?* If not well, what exactly is hindering the view? What sin do you need to excise from your life in order to have a more grand, more glorious view of your God? If your conception of God is lackluster, it is no fault of his. If God does not seem glorious and good to you, you are not looking hard enough.

Seeing God Soon

In the Bible, the Christian's ultimate hope is often summarized as seeing God. This is what we yearn for. "For now we see in a mirror dimly, but then face to face" (1 Cor. 13:12). The reward for the pure in heart is that, at long last, they are given the thing they have long pursued. Those who make God their sole delight in this life will be eternally satisfied with his actual presence in the next life. Nothing could be better! "As for me, I shall behold your face in righteousness," David writes. "When I awake, I shall be satisfied with your likeness" (Ps. 17:15). This is why that moment has been called the beatific vision—literally, the sight that makes us happy. Jonathan Edwards once wrote, "The glorious excellencies and beauty of God will be what will forever entertain the minds of the saints."[9] I love that way of putting it—"forever *entertain*." We will never grow bored of beholding Christ. It's remarkable how we can become accustomed to splendor and beauty. People will spend millions of dollars on a beachfront property, but then in no time at all they'll take the amazing view for granted. A trip to the Louvre is a once-in-a-lifetime opportunity for art-lovers to see pieces like *Mona Lisa* or *Venus de Milo*; for the security guards, those works of art have become mere decorations at the office. We will never take Jesus for granted in glory. We will never yawn in heaven, or check our phones, or glance at our watches, or peer around to see if there's something better to do. With our sins removed, with our vision at long last unclouded, we will everlastingly adore that which is perfectly adorable. We will finally "dwell in the house of the LORD ... to gaze upon the beauty of the LORD" (Ps. 27:4). Peter expressed well our hope: "Though you have not seen him, you love him. Though you do not now see him, you believe in him and rejoice with joy that is inexpressible and filled with glory" (1 Peter 1:8).

There's one other thing: This sight will be *transformative*. Moses's face shone just from getting a glimpse of God's goodness. When we behold God's glory in the face of Jesus Christ, we will become glorious. "Those who look to him are radiant," says David (Ps. 34:5), and John writes with even more detail that "when he appears we shall be like him, because we shall see him as he is" (1 John 3:2). We will become what we behold. It is not until we

---

9. Jonathan Edwards, "God Glorified in Man's Dependence," in *The Works of Jonathan Edwards* (1834; repr., Hendrickson, 2000), 2:5.

see God that we will be what we were always meant to be—what a blessing is bound up in this beatitude!

CONCLUSION

In the end, the sixth beatitude is not merely an invitation to moral discipline; it's a call to wholehearted devotion. Jesus reminds us that the essence of the Christian life is found not in outward performance but in inward transformation—a heart undivided and wholly set on God. To be pure in heart is to desire one thing above all others: to see God. And that's the very thing we get! Heart-purity is in itself a reward—how wonderful to live a life unencumbered by idolatrous pursuits or competing desires! But to the gospel grace of sanctification God also attaches the promise of future glorification. Let us then give ourselves wholly to this pursuit of purity, knowing that the reward is not only the cleanness of our hearts but the joy of beholding the face of our God forever. Dear reader, don't grow discouraged. Your sincerity and simplicity of heart will be rewarded. You will see God.

FOR FURTHER REFLECTION

1. How would you explain to someone what it means to be "pure in heart"?
2. In a world that says, "Follow your heart," how is Jesus's call to purity of heart both radically countercultural and liberating?
3. How is it paradoxical that those who most clearly see the holiness of God are also those who are most painfully aware of their own impurity? How does this lead to peace and joy, not despair?

4. Why is "seeing God" the promised blessing for the pure in heart? What does this tell us about the connection between sanctification and communion with God?
5. What are some common signs that our hearts have become distracted, divided, or dulled in their devotion to God? How might we begin to "purify" them again by grace? What practical steps can you take to guard and cultivate purity of heart this week?

7
HEAVENLY RESEMBLANCE

Blessed are the peacemakers, for they shall be called sons of God.
MATTHEW 5:9

Few things more adorn and beautify a Christian profession than exercising and manifesting the spirit of peace.
A. W. PINK

IN JULY 1969, John Lennon and his new wife Yoko Ono released their first song together: the anti-war anthem "Give Peace a Chance." After a series of absurdist verses, the song settles into the repetition of "All we are saying is give peace a chance." The line came to John when he was being interviewed during the couple's famous "bed-in," a weeks-long protest during which they remained in their bed and pajamas. "What's the point?" inquired a reporter. "We're just trying to give peace a chance," said John. The song was an instant hit and has remained popular ever since.

At first glance, it might sound like Jesus and Lennon are singing the same song when our Lord says, "Blessed are the peacemakers," but that couldn't be further from the truth. Jesus isn't applauding people for giving a thumbs-up to peace. He isn't commending those who think peace is a pretty great idea. He isn't even promising blessing to the peace*ful* or peace*able*. Jesus's word of blessing is for peace*makers*. The blessed aren't idealists lying in bed and telling others, "Hey, let's give peace a chance." The blessed are realists who get out of bed and do something about it.[1]

THE PURSUIT OF PEACE

Contrary to common belief, peacemaking is not passive. In fact, God's Word tells us in four different places that peace is a *pursuit*:

> So then let us pursue what makes for peace and for mutual upbuilding. (Rom. 14:19)

---

1. D. A. Carson, *Jesus's Sermon on the Mount and His Confrontation with the World: A Study of Matthew 5–10* (Baker Books, 2018), 32.

> So flee youthful passions and pursue righteousness, faith, love, and peace, along with those who call on the Lord from a pure heart. (2 Tim. 2:22)
>
> Let him turn away from evil and do good; let him seek peace and pursue it. (1 Peter 3:11 [quoting from Ps. 34:14])
>
> Pursue peace with all people, and holiness, without which no one will see the Lord. (Heb. 12:14 NKJV)

This teaches us that peace doesn't just fall into our laps—not in a world where every interpersonal relationship is broken, fractured, or fragile to some degree because of sin and selfishness. Of course, if you find yourself in a home marked by tranquility, or a church community that naturally gets along with little to no conflict, thank God. "Behold, how good and pleasant it is when brothers dwell in unity!" (Ps. 133:1). But since that is not the norm, peace is something we must diligently pursue.

Interestingly, the word used in the New Testament for "pursue" is the same word used in the very next beatitude: "Blessed are those who are *persecuted* for righteousness' sake" (Matt. 5:10). To pursue is to go after something with such an unrelenting determination that—when done in a certain way—it could rightly be called persecution. It doesn't mean sitting in bed and writing songs about that thing. Is peace your unflagging pursuit?

What Pursuing Peace Is Not

Pursuing peace is not avoiding conflict. It isn't shrinking back from difficult conversations. Ken Sande has helpfully called this sort of escapist approach "peace-faking."[2] But if there's one thing Jesus

---

2. Ken Sande, *The Peacemaker: A Biblical Guide to Resolving Personal Conflict*

is abundantly clear about in the Sermon on the Mount, it is that no one can "fake it" in his kingdom: "For I tell you, unless your righteousness exceeds that of the scribes and Pharisees, you will never enter the kingdom of heaven" (Matt. 5:20). The faithful disciple of Christ is not just a peaceable person, one who refrains from fits of rage or brooding resentment—though this must be true! But Jesus requires even more from us. He calls us, as peacemakers, to step into the midst of conflict, not to stand back and watch it from a distance. Just as a policeman does little good if he passively watches a crime unfold with the justification "I am a man of law; I cannot be involved with criminality," so too a peacemaker is one in name only if they see a relational fire and do nothing to put it out.

Now, let me be clear: Pursuing peace is not feeding our insatiable need to always get our way or to silence every opposing view. That is "peace-breaking."[3] It seems to me that many professing believers forget this when they log into their social media accounts. If posts and comment sections are any indication, Christians often assume that whoever says it the loudest or the wittiest wins. The path to peace looks like little more than silencing and shaming one's opponent. Peace-faking sacrifices truth at the altar of love; peace-breaking sacrifices love at the altar of truth. Peacemaking, on the other hand, refuses to sacrifice either.

What Pursuing Peace Is

Peacemakers apply the truth of God's Word with the love and gentleness of God's Spirit to all their relationships. While they will never sacrifice truth or love, they will, following in the steps of Jesus, sacrifice themselves: "If possible, *so far as it depends on*

(Baker, 2004), 28.
3. Sande, 28.

you, live peaceably with all" (Rom. 12:18). Paul's instructions in Ephesians 4 are really helpful here:

> Rather, speaking the truth in love, we are to grow up in every way into him who is the head, into Christ. . . .
>
> Therefore, having put away falsehood, let each one of you speak the truth with his neighbor, for we are members one of another. Be angry and do not sin; do not let the sun go down on your anger, and give no opportunity to the devil. . . . Let no corrupting talk come out of your mouths, but only such as is good for building up, as fits the occasion, that it may give grace to those who hear. (Eph. 4:15, 25–27, 29)

Paul teaches us that Christians prize and prioritize the truth in all their speech, having completely put away falsehood. However, they don't do this to win arguments or prove themselves right; they do it to communicate love and grace to those who hear them. To speak truth with ill intent or anger gives an "opportunity to the devil," the great hater and enemy of peace. God's method for peacemaking requires a loving commitment to his Word—the true guide for all our conduct and relationships.

The peace that the Bible knows is all about gentleness, sacrifice, forgiveness, reconciliation, and restoration. Peacemakers address sin redemptively. They not only look at a broken situation and say, "This is wrong," but also ask, "How can I make it better?" Terry Johnson calls peacemakers "agents of reconciliation."[4] They eagerly apply the transformative grace of the gospel to every conflict,

---

4. Terry L. Johnson, *When Grace Transforms: The Character of Christ's Disciples Put Forward in the Beatitudes* (Christian Focus, 2002), 107.

trusting that the Lord will use it to mend fractured relationships with peace and unity.

Why Pursuing Peace Is Hard

The greatest obstacle to pursuing peace, it needs to be said, is our own hearts. Richard Baxter was a pastor during a time of great upheaval in the Church of England, and he reflected often on the need for Christian unity and concord. Once he said, "I dare presume to take it for granted, that all you that hear me this day, would fain have divisions taken away, and have unity, and concord, and peace through the world.... *But you little think that it is you, and such as you, that are the hinderers of it.*"[5]

I find that convicting. Peacemaking isn't just about how I address the sins of those people out there; it's first and foremost about how I address the sin in my own heart. Conflict usually involves sin on both sides, but we are often tempted to look for sin on the other side first. Just as we are prone to think the grass on the other side is greener, we tend to think the sin on the other side is darker. But the sin Jesus asks peacemakers to find first is their own. Jesus's later teaching in the Sermon on the Mount about the speck and the log in the eye applies well here (see Matt. 7:1–4). As James writes,

> What causes quarrels and what causes fights among you? Is it not this, that your passions are at war within you? You desire and do not have, so you murder. You covet and cannot obtain, so you fight and quarrel. (James 4:1–2)

---

5. Richard Baxter, *Christian Unity*, Lexham Classics (1830; repr., Lexham, 2017), 90. Emphasis mine.

There could be many reasons for the lack of peace we experience, but the first place to look is our own hearts.

Pursuing peace, therefore, means searching out our thoughts, affections, and behaviors. We cannot pursue peace without until we have pursued it within. It requires vulnerable and self-searching prayers, like

> Search me, O God, and know my heart!
> Try me and know my thoughts!
> And see if there be any grievous way in me,
> and lead me in the way everlasting! (Ps. 139:23–24)

We will quickly find that there are sins we must repent of and behaviors we must change in order to make peace in our homes, in our marriages, in our relationships, and in our churches. When we say that we are all about peacemaking but refuse to examine ourselves, we are not pursuing peace; we are merely paying lip service to it. Peacemaking is a humbling and difficult endeavor, but it is one that Jesus blesses—and, by God's grace, it is actually attainable.

THE PRESERVATION OF PEACE

Scripture commands us not only to pursue peace but also to preserve it. Paul says we should be "eager to maintain the unity of the Spirit in the bond of peace" (Eph. 4:3). In other words, it isn't enough to make peace; we must then maintain it. How? Paul's command actually provides a clue: We must cherish the unity that we receive from the Holy Spirit. What brings the Christian community together isn't that we bite our tongues and force ourselves to get along with one another. It's that there is a supernatural bond holding us together. That's an objective reality, and our desire as

Christ's disciples should be to experience it subjectively. We want brothers and sisters in the Lord to agree because, well, *they are in the Lord.*

So, we maintain peace by majoring on the majors. It is often minor issues and trivial annoyances that cause disunity. Do we need to let someone else's strongly held opinions on parenting disrupt our fellowship with them? What about stark differences in hobbies or interests? What about when we have nothing in common with each other? The answer to all these questions is no, and we won't allow such things to separate us from fellow Christians if we keep in mind that they are our blood-bought siblings in Christ. Most political differences, even if adamantly held, shouldn't threaten the unity that Christians are called to enjoy either. Though our tendency is to back away from that which is different, the Bible calls us to lean in. The church of God is a people who are cemented tightly together—not despite their differences but even on account of them. We love and treasure the beauty of the Spirit that is displayed in a diversity of gifts (see 1 Cor. 12:4–11). What other society operates in such a way? This is one of the unique privileges of belonging to Christ's kingdom. But if we aren't careful, the smallest cracks will become the largest chasms.

We will maintain peace when we keep the Maker of our unity the center of our unity.[6] When you face a situation that may lead to trouble, pause. Don't speak; think. Ask yourself, "What is at stake here? What does the Bible say about this? How does the gospel come to bear on this situation? How can I best honor Christ in this?" If we don't take that sanctified moment to pause and reflect, our first thought when trouble comes will often be "What must

---

6. Baxter writes, "O Christians, keep close to Christ the center of your unity, and the Scripture, which is the rule of it, and cherish the Spirit which is the vital cause [of it]." Baxter, 147.

I do to get my way in this situation?" As long as we stand at the center, Christ will drift to the periphery. When Christ is displaced in our hearts and relationships, we will fail to preserve peace. But when we keep him in the center, he and his gospel exert a centripetal force that will hold us all together.

Above all else, peacemakers and maintainers will be men and women of prayer, people who seek the Lord's help in this great task. Christ's power created our peace, and only his power can preserve it. "Apart from me you can do nothing," Jesus told us (John 15:5). That includes making and maintaining peace, and so we are driven to pray. John Bunyan once gave this wise counsel to his congregation: "If ever we would live in peace and unity we must pray for it. We are required to seek peace; of whom, then, can we seek it with expectation to find it but of him who is a God of peace, and hath promised to bless his people with peace?"[7] In the absence of prayer, no amount of tips, tricks, or steps will ever produce a true peacemaker. The fruit of the Spirit is peace (see Gal. 5:22), so we must pray that that same Spirit would produce it and preserve it in our lives and our various relations.

THE MAKER OF PEACE

What's thrilling about the work of peacemaking, and hopefully a great motivation for us to get to it, is that peacemakers walk in the very footsteps of God. God is *the* great Peacemaker. This is the undeniable truth of Scripture. As creator, God literally made peace in this world. He took what was void and empty and created

---

7. John Bunyan, *The Complete Works of John Bunyan* (1692; repr., The National Foundation for Christian Education, 1968), 3:402.

perfection and wholeness. The world was made to be a harmonious home—not only for Adam and Eve but for mankind and Maker to dwell in peaceful fellowship.

Sin ripped an ugly tear in the beautiful fabric of God's peaceful world. Immediately Adam and Eve knew conflict, a conflict passed down to their first two sons. Most tragically, though, by choosing sin, man forfeited harmony with God. But that is not the end of the story. The rest of it is all about God's own unflagging pursuit of peace. This is the gospel story, isn't it? There's a reason the angels were singing, "Peace on earth!" at the incarnation: This is why Christ came! It is through Christ that we who were once enemies have been reconciled to God (see Rom. 5:10). We now have "peace with God through our Lord Jesus Christ" (Rom. 5:1)!

Because sin disrupted our relationship with God, the New Testament authors can hardly speak of the work of Christ without connecting it to the concept of peace. Ours is a "gospel of peace" (Eph. 6:15) because Christ "himself is our peace" (Eph 2:14), the one who "preached peace" (Eph. 2:17). He is the "Prince of Peace" (Isa. 9:6), the Son of one who is repeatedly called "the God of peace" (Rom. 15:33; 16:20; Phil. 4:9; 1 Thess. 5:23; Heb. 13:20). Christ comes as the light of God to "guide our feet into the way of peace" (Luke 1:79). Through the cruel violence of Calvary, Jesus was "making peace by the blood of his cross" (Col. 1:20).

Did you catch that? The gospel is about Jesus "making peace." What does he do in this beatitude? He invites his disciples to follow in the course he has already charted. To mirror him. To join in his glorious gospel work. No wonder there is blessing in this! Peacemakers "are doing the very work which the Son of God began when he came to earth the first time, and which he will finish when he returns the second time."[8] Paul tells the Christians in Rome, "The God of peace will soon crush Satan under *your* feet" (Rom. 16:20). The God of peace invites us to share in the peacemaking work of the Son, which includes giving the final death blow to the master of division and disunity. The meek, mild, and peacemaking followers of Christ will utterly crush and vanquish the Evil One—how's that for a paradox! But it's the same paradox that is at the heart of the gospel: Jesus, the man of peace, is at the same time the great warrior who comes to do battle for his people.

MADE LIKE THE MAKER

In this light, the promise attached to this beatitude makes good sense: "Blessed are the peacemakers, *for they shall be called sons of God.*" It is perfectly fitting for those who do the work of the Son to share in the name of the Son as well! In Hebrew thought, the term *son* implies resemblance in character or similarity in status.[9] Jesus says that peacemakers will be called the "sons of God" because they will resemble their Father, who is the God of Peace, and their Elder Brother, who is the Prince of Peace.

That's a rare thing in this world. Here we have, yet again, the upside-down, inside-out nature of Christ's kingdom. This is the only kingdom in all of human history where the citizens are called not to make war but to make peace. Do you remember how Peter learned that lesson? His sword was still dripping with blood as Jesus healed the wound he inflicted, saying, "No more of this" (Luke 22:51). Says Matthew Henry, "Christ never intended to

---

8. J. C. Ryle, *Matthew: Expository Thoughts on the Gospels* (Banner of Truth, 2012), 28.
9. For a less flattering example, Jesus uses the phrase "sons of the evil one" to refer to people who behave like the devil (Matt. 13:38).

have his religion propagated by fire and sword, or penal laws, or to acknowledge bigotry, or intemperate zeal, as the mark of his disciples."[10] While earthly kings (and their citizens) find meaning through land grabs, trade wars, and power plays, the mark of a heavenly citizen—indeed, a true child of God—is peacemaking.

I like to wear bow ties most Sundays when I'm preaching. (Please do not judge, and just keep reading.) My son wears them, too. So, he looks like his father. But here's the deal: *We make him wear the bow ties!* I don't think he would if it were up to him. Yet there are other things he does without even thinking twice—certain patterns of speech, facial expressions, and the like—that are completely natural to him and that are nearly identical to me. It's those behaviors that often elicit this response from a smiling older saint: "He *really is* his father's son!"

Peacemaking is that sort of confirmation, both to ourselves and to those who are watching us. We confirm our sonship when we do what our Father in heaven does and loves best, and that includes making peace. When we put down our proud sword and instead take up our humble cross, the world will notice. When we resist the urge to pursue our own interests or assert our rights, when we do not crush others to climb the ladder of success, when we take no interest in standing tallest or shouting loudest but instead care first and foremost that wounds are healed, sins forgiven, and relationships restored, we point people to Christ, to God himself. People will see us and call us sons and daughters of God, those who resemble their heavenly Father.

But ultimately, the one calling peacemakers the sons of God is God himself. That is what Jesus is saying here. "Blessed are the

---

10. Matthew Henry, *Commentary on the Whole Bible* (Hendrickson, 1996), 5:42.

peacemakers, for God claims them as his own sons." The hope of the previous beatitude was the chance to see God. It's hard to imagine something greater than that—but there is, and this is it. Here we learn that we will see God as our Father, and he will see us as his children. Could there be anything better? We now hold this declaration from the Lord near and dear to our hearts, but one day it will be declared to the whole world. On the day when all fighting ceases, when all conflict is over, when all shall be peace, God will say, "You are my child."

CONCLUSION

"Give peace a chance" might make for a good anti-war slogan, but it's also anti-gospel. The gospel is not about a hypothetical peace that maybe could be attained; it's about a decisive peace that Christ won for us at the cost of his own life. And his sacrifice of love doesn't give us an option: We *must* live as ambassadors of peace in this broken world, ready to pursue it at any cost. That cost will likely be our convenience and our comfort. We need to examine the secret evils of our hearts, die to self, and run into the fray to bring about peace. That is hard, even scary, work. But there is no conflict, no chaos, no fight, no turmoil so great that it can make us tremble if we remember this: "He owns me for his child; I can no longer fear."[11]

FOR FURTHER REFLECTION

1. Why do you think Jesus attaches the identity "sons of God" to this particular beatitude? What does that reveal about God's character and mission?

11. Charles Wesley, "Arise, My Soul, Arise!" 1742.

2. How do our common conceptions of peace regularly collide with the biblical work of peacemaking?
3. What do you find are the greatest threats to peace in your own life? What about the greatest barriers to peacemaking?
4. How does the gospel uniquely equip believers to make peace in a way that secular approaches to conflict resolution cannot?
5. Where in your life right now is God calling you to step toward reconciliation? What would obedience to that call look like?

8

THROUGH MANY DANGERS, TOILS, AND SNARES

Blessed are those who are persecuted for righteousness' sake, for theirs is the kingdom of heaven. Blessed are you when others revile you and persecute you and utter all kinds of evil against you falsely on my account. Rejoice and be glad, for your reward is great in heaven, for so they persecuted the prophets who were before you.

MATTHEW 5:10-12

If you have experienced even a glimpse of the glory of the things in the Kingdom of Heaven and regard them as certain and real, how easy would it be for you to endure anything in the world.

JEREMIAH BURROUGHS

IT'S SURPRISING ENOUGH that Jesus would call the persecuted life the blessed life; it's even more surprising that he does so *twice*. In fact, this is the only blessing that Jesus takes the time to repeat. The first statement in verse 10 follows the standard formula we have come to expect: "Blessed are the/those . . ." But then in verses 11–12, Jesus doubles down, stating *again* that there is blessing in persecution.

What are we to make of this repetition and emphasis? I think two things need to be said. First, when taken together, the Bible's frequent teaching on the subject must mean that for Christians, persecution is the norm, not the exception. Jesus said emphatically, "If they persecuted me, they will also persecute you" (John 15:20). A theme of Paul and Barnabas's missional preaching was that "through many tribulations we must enter the kingdom of God" (Acts 14:22). In 1 Timothy 3:12 we find this definitive statement: "Indeed, all who desire to live a godly life in Christ Jesus will be persecuted." Christ's kingdom is so countercultural that it elicits cold and sometimes harsh pushback, not a warm embrace. That is how radically different the way of Christ is from the way of the world: You shouldn't expect the world to go along with it.

There's a second reason why I think Jesus, and the Bible as a whole, stresses the reality of persecution: We are so prone to misinterpret its purpose. When persecution comes, our natural instinct is to doubt the goodness of a God who permits such suffering. Though we are certainly not meant to enjoy suffering and persecution, neither are we to interpret them as things of ultimate evil. We are to draw near to God through persecutions, which won't happen if we grow to distrust the One who sends them.

So, let's take a look at these verses and reacquaint ourselves with the Bible's teaching on this important subject. We will do so by asking three questions: What kind of persecution is Jesus speaking of, why are we to rejoice during it, and how could we possibly persevere through it?

WHAT KIND OF PERSECUTION?

The kind of persecution that Jesus describes is one that comes in direct response to living the counterLtural lifestyle he has been describing. This helps us understand why this beatitude lands where it does in the list: It comes last because it is the expected outcome of living according to Christ's commands. It is those who are poor in spirit, who mourn their condition, who are meek before others, who hunger and thirst after righteousness, who devote themselves to a pure love for God, and who strive to make peace in the world who will be persecuted.

That means this is not a promised blessing for anyone who ever happens to be mistreated or persecuted for any reason. Though God has a heart for those who suffer at the hands of the unjust and cruel, that isn't the emphasis of this beatitude. It's speaking in the narrow sense of *Christian* persecution. To be clear, by "Christian" persecution, I don't mean any instance in which a Christian is being treated poorly; I mean instances in which a Christian is specifically persecuted *for being a Christian*. Christians can receive ill treatment, but sometimes it's our own fault. Sometimes we bring it on ourselves because our behavior is objectionable, unreasonable, rude, or unkind. That would be persecution for *our* sake, or on *our* account. Jesus speaks of persecution for *righteousness'* sake and on *his* account.

In a similar way, Scripture calls Christ the "rock of offense" (see, for example, 1 Peter 2:8), but it never permits Christians to be offensive. Our message is offensive enough. If we are persecuted on account of the message, then there is blessing. If we are persecuted on account of how we present the message, then we will find no solace in these verses. If we are to be persecuted, it needs to be because we are associated with Christ and his kingdom, not because we act contrary to them.

So, we don't want to be persecuted for the *wrong* thing, but are we ready and willing to be persecuted for the *right* thing? What might that look like? Are we willing to make a stand against ungodly policies at work, or resist the sway of contemporary culture, or turn away from the impure pursuits of our unbelieving friends, even if it will mean ostracism, ridicule, or worse? The ancient church father Tertullian dealt with this same concern in his pastorate. One of his parishioners had a conflict between his business interests and his faith in Jesus. As he recounted the issue to Pastor Tertullian, he concluded by saying, "What am I to do? After all, I must live." Tertullian replied, "Must you?"[1] When persecution comes, our commitments are tested. At one point in our lives, we professed faith in Christ and said, "I have decided to follow Jesus! No turning back, no turning back!" And yet the road we have left in our wake probably has never looked so alluring as when the grim shadow of persecution looms before us. But if we are following Jesus, that shadow is actually a sign that we are headed in the right direction.

---

1. Quoted in James Montgomery Boice, *The Sermon on the Mount* (Zondervan, 1972), 60.

WHY ARE WE TO REJOICE?

According to this beatitude, we are to press on even in the face of persecution—and to do so with joy! Our response is to rejoice! Hardly a natural response, but entirely expected if we have picked up on the paradoxical message of the Beatitudes. John Stott explains well the kind of response that Jesus expects of his followers: "We are not to retaliate like an unbeliever, nor to sulk like a child, nor to lick our wounds in self-pity like a dog, nor just to grin and bear it like a Stoic, still less to pretend we enjoy it like a masochist. What then? We are to rejoice as a Christian should rejoice and even to 'leap for joy.'"[2] What explains this surprising response? What truths do we need to take hold of to manifest it ourselves? I think three helps emerge from the text.

First, we are to rejoice when persecuted because persecution confirms our faith as genuine, and the assurance of faith is a more precious gift than persecution is a painful loss (see 1 Peter 1:7). Jesus says, "Rejoice and be glad . . . for so they persecuted the prophets who were before you." If we are persecuted, "we belong to a noble succession."[3] The devil turns his minions on those who are actually making a difference, those whose faith is vibrant and alluring to others. He so desires to snuff out that light before others are drawn to it.

Here's a paradox. As Christians, we must remember that negative feedback is just as likely to indicate success as failure. The prophets in the Old Testament were persecuted because they brought not a message tailored to the fancies of the day but a message of truth. The world's reviling confirms that what we believe

---

2. John R. W. Stott, *Christian Counter-Culture: The Message of the Sermon on the Mount*, The Bible Speaks Today (InterVarsity Press, 1978), 52.
3. Stott, 52.

and profess is not man's message but God's. Suffering authenticates the divine identity of the message's true Author.

Second, we must rejoice when persecuted because persecution draws us into closer communion with Christ. The less we have of the world's favor and fellowship, the more we have of Christ's. The apostles took the message they heard Jesus preaching in this beatitude and put it into practice. They were beaten by the Sanhedrin for preaching the gospel, and in response to the bruises, they went out "rejoicing that they were counted worthy to suffer dishonor for the name" (Acts 5:41). What an astounding statement. They were honored to be dishonored, since such dishonor was on account of their Savior. Why? They did not view their persecution as a sign that God had forgotten them, but rather as one that God had promoted them! They felt supremely dignified that they could be bruised and bloodied for the Savior who was bruised and bloodied for them. What a privilege to know the Suffering Servant in such a unique way—to know more deeply his pain, follow more closely his path, sense more keenly his love, be conformed more fully to his image.

Others throughout the history of the church have been called to similar suffering and have similarly rejoiced. The second-century bishop named Polycarp was threatened with ravenous lions if he would not recant the faith. When that proved fruitless, he was instead burned. Moments before the spire was lit, he prayed, "I bless thee, that thou hast granted me this day and hour, that I may share, among the number of the martyrs, in the cup of thy Christ."[4] He likewise considered his persecution a privilege, as it afforded him a moment to share more deeply in his fellowship

---

4. "The Martyrdom of Polycarp," in *The Apostolic Fathers*, trans. Kirsopp Lake (William Heinemann, 1917), 2:331.

with Christ. George Wishart, a Scottish Reformer, was hanged and then burned in 1546. He's recorded as saying, "For the Word's sake I suffer this day by men, not sorrowfully, but with a glad heart and mind." John Rogers, the very first English Protestant executed under the persecutions of Queen "Bloody" Mary, was burned at the stake in 1555. He walked with such joy to his death that it was thought he could have been walking to his wedding.[5]

There are countless saints who have shared this same way of thinking but who will never make it into the history books. There is the wedding photographer who loses his business for not accepting a gig for a same-sex union; there is the professor who voluntarily walks away from her beloved career and calling rather than abide by a new pronoun policy; there is the husband who endures ridicule for his faith from his unbelieving wife but nevertheless serves her lovingly and joyfully. Is Jesus so precious and dear to us that we would rejoice in suffering and scorn if they brought us closer to him?

A third reason we are to rejoice when persecuted is because Jesus promises us we will be greatly rewarded. Considering how intense, relentless, and even fatal persecution can be, we need to really understand the nature of this reward for it to give us joy. Don't wait for trouble to come and then hope you will be able to cling to the hope of your reward then. Understand your reward now, and you will be ready and courageous to face any danger that the world or the devil can throw at you. What Jesus offers us is *heavenly*. He repeats the opening blessing from the first beatitude, "theirs is the kingdom of heaven," which reminds us that all the Beatitudes have been pointing us beyond this world and toward

---

5. See Mack Tomlinson, "John Rogers of England," Banner of Truth, March 2, 2005, https://banneroftruth.org/us/resources/articles/2005/john-rogers-of-england/.

heaven. Jesus is preparing us to live as faithful citizens in this world, and that will always entail a firm reminder that our true and ultimate citizenship is in heaven (see Phil. 3:20).

To say that our reward is heavenly is not only to say that it is future, or that it is certain, but that is better. Jesus underscores this, doesn't he? "Rejoice and be glad, for your reward is *great* in heaven." Things in heaven are better than things on earth. What Christ is offering is better than treasure, better than fame, better than health, better than long life, better than close friends, better than peace and safety. The greatest good on earth is nothing in comparison to the least good in heaven, were there such a thing.

HOW CAN WE PERSEVERE?

The reward that awaits us in glory isn't just a reason for immense joy, but it's also one of the greatest motivators of unwavering perseverance in the face of persecution. Setting our minds on that which is above is really the key to keep us going on when we are tempted to despair (see Col. 3:1–4). Thomas Watson has this great line: "Look upon the crown, *and faint if you can*."[6] In other words, if we could see our reward in heaven, we would be so animated with joy and courage and thanksgiving to God that we couldn't fear the trials in this life even if we tried.

According to the author of Hebrews, this heavenly mindset allowed Moses to endure amid persecution. Moses could have enjoyed the pleasures of being a prince in Pharaoh's house. Instead, he chose to associate with the people of Israel, the miserable lot suffering under the persecution of Egyptian elitism and tyranny.

---

6. Thomas Watson, *The Beatitudes: An Exposition of Matthew 5:1–10* (repr., Banner of Truth, 1980), 295. Emphasis mine.

Why? "He considered the reproach of Christ greater wealth than the treasures of Egypt, for he was looking to the reward" (Heb. 11:26). Moses was looking to his reward, and we are called to do so as well. When we do, we will see that bearing reproach for Christ is actually worth more than all the treasures of the world. That's because suffering with Christ brings heavenly blessings. A Christian who is in the worst condition imaginable—called to die a painful death for their faith—is blessed. They are soon to be in possession of more treasures than all the wealth of every earthly kingdom throughout all history combined. The worst thing that can happen to us only makes us better: Death leads to glory.

Most significantly, Jesus himself used this method as he faced the greatest persecution and suffering of all, and we are meant to emulate him:

> Therefore, since we are surrounded by so great a cloud of witnesses, let us also lay aside every weight, and sin which clings so closely, and let us run with endurance the race that is set before us, looking to Jesus, the founder and perfecter of our faith, who for the joy that was set before him endured the cross, despising the shame, and is seated at the right hand of the throne of God. (Heb. 12:1–2)

What was the joy that was set before Jesus? He rejoiced to know that by his sufferings he would make peace between God and man, that he would accomplish the work he had come to do, that he would soon be with his Father in glory, and that he would bring with him all his chosen people. We all will likewise have a cross to bear in this life. It is very possible, dear reader, that your cross will entail being mocked, beaten, or even killed for your faith in Christ. When that cross appears, what joy will enable you to endure it? It is the joy of sins forgiven, the joy of tears wiped away, the joy of sighs completed, the joy of suffering done. It is the joy of happiness restored. It is the joy of frustrations frustrated and of death defeated. Above all, our joy is that we will dwell in the house of the Lord forevermore. Our reward in heaven is him. We will have Christ—*forever*. A forever like that will bolster and buoy you amid "this light momentary affliction" (2 Cor. 4:17).

Moreover, when we look to Christ above, we see not only the crown that he will give us but also the scars that he bears for us. We see the wounds he endured, and we're reminded of the persecution that he underwent on our behalf. A sober estimation of the sufferings of Christ will steel us for our own sufferings. The author of Hebrews goes on to say, "Consider him who endured from sinners such hostility against himself, so that you may not grow weary or fainthearted" (12:3). Our troubles will seem slight, manageable, and even joyful in the kingdom of God when we consider his.

CONCLUSION

This beatitude reminds me of Aleksandr Solzhenitsyn, the Soviet-era author and activist. Though he wasn't imprisoned for his faith, it was in prison that he came to faith. In a cruel Soviet gulag, a kindly doctor witnessed to him during his treatments for cancer, and as a result, he was converted. Solzhenitsyn later wrote, "I turn back to the years of my imprisonment and say, sometimes to the astonishment of those about me: 'Bless you, prison! . . . Bless you, prison, for having been my life!'"[7]

7. Aleksandr Solzhenitsyn, *The Gulag Archipelago, 1918–1956: An Experiment in Literary Investigation*, trans. Thomas P. Whitney and Harry Willetts, abr. Edward E. Ericson Jr. (Perennial, 1983), 313.

"Bless you, prison!" is a statement as seemingly absurd as "Bless you, persecution!" How can blessings be found in such dark places or be given to such lowly people? But that's what Christ says here, and by blessing the persecuted he is guaranteeing that the persecutions themselves are *his* ministers; they perform his bidding, not the devil's. Just as a prison cell can be the place of salvation, persecution can be—and, for the Christian, *will* be—the means of blessing. This beatitude ensures that our struggles will be sanctified, resulting in glorious bliss. The world thinks there is blessing in the ease of popularity and the security of power. But God has placed it elsewhere: in mourning, meekness, and even reproach. According to Jesus, the sorriest people in the eyes of the world are, in point of fact, the happiest.

FOR FURTHER REFLECTION

1. This chapter emphasizes that for Christians "persecution is the norm, not the exception." How does this statement challenge or confirm your current understanding of the Christian life in a non-Christian world?
2. What specific scenarios in your life or community might test your willingness to suffer for Christ, and how can you prepare for such moments?
3. How can we possibly rejoice while we are suffering? What else does the Bible have to say on this subject?
4. How can believers discern whether the challenges they face are due to their faith or to their foolish actions, and why is this distinction crucial?
5. How does the historical experience of Christian persecution, as described in this chapter, inform and encourage believers facing challenges today?

Conclusion

PARADOX PEOPLE

> You are the salt of the earth, but if salt has lost its taste, how shall its saltiness be restored? It is no longer good for anything except to be thrown out and trampled under people's feet. You are the light of the world. A city set on a hill cannot be hidden. Nor do people light a lamp and put it under a basket, but on a stand, and it gives light to all in the house. In the same way, let your light shine before others, so that they may see your good works and give glory to your Father who is in heaven.
>
> **MATTHEW 5:13–16**

> I feel there are two things it is impossible to desire with sufficient ardor—personal holiness and the honor of Christ in the salvation of souls.
>
> **ROBERT MURRAY M'CHEYNE**

"THE MAN WITH THE GOLDEN ARM." No, that's not the name of a Bond villain. It's the nickname Australian James Harrison earned as he became the most prolific blood and plasma donor of all time. It was discovered that his blood contained rare and powerful antibodies against the Rh D antigen, which is the cause of a fatal disease in newborns known as rhesus. From age eighteen until his death at age eighty-eight, Harrison gladly donated blood every two weeks, and he's credited with saving the lives of over two million infants. From his perspective, all he did was sit in a chair. An ordinary act, yet the results were anything but.[1]

Do you believe that the ordinary faithfulness of a Christian can be used by God in extraordinary ways? We might assent to this doctrinally, but it's hard to do so practically. Many of us live with the irrepressible suspicion that we need to *do* something significant or *be* someone special in order to impact the world around us. In our studies of the Beatitudes, we have consistently encountered the struggle to trust that the virtues Christ is calling us to are actually blessed. To suggest that meekness or purity of heart are on the road to great success and satisfaction is so countercultural that it's hard to accept. In fact, it's more than countercultural; it's counterintuitive. It goes against the grain of our own hearts. As those who are in the world but never to be conformed to it, we need to constantly recalibrate our hearts and minds to ensure we are operating according to heavenly principles. The surprising

---

1. Rachel Treisman, "James Harrison, Whose Blood Donations Saved over 2 Million Babies, Has Died," NPR, March 3, 2025, https://www.npr.org/2025/03/03/nx-s1-5316163/james-harrison-blood-donor.

message of the Beatitudes is a good corrective to that end, but perhaps the greatest twist of all is this: Not only are these virtues the way we attain blessings for ourselves, but they are the God-appointed means by which we can bestow blessings on others.

USEFUL CHRISTIANS

That is what Jesus teaches in the verses immediately following the Beatitudes. After establishing what kingdom character *is*, he then tells us what it *does* (and it does do something!). Jesus draws out this truth using two metaphors: Christians who live out the Beatitudes are like salt and light. There is nothing exotic about salt or luxurious about light, but they are useful. God loves to use ordinary things in extraordinary ways (see 1 Cor. 1:26–29). Faithful church attendance, regular family devotions, persistent prayer, godly conduct in the workplace, self-denial, cross-bearing—these are the sorts of tools the Lord loves to work with. Here is the ultimate paradox for the people of God: It is the simplest things that God uses in the biggest way. Living a holy life, though a far cry from glamorous, is nothing short of glorious. God's saints are how he glorifies himself in the world. Indeed, Jesus tells us here that we lead others to give the Lord glory through our good works (see also John 13:35). Holiness is the highest good a Christian can offer the society they are living in.

And Christians *are* to do good for society. Both of these metaphors draw out explicitly what the Beatitudes have taught implicitly: We have both a responsibility and a relationship to the world. A camouflage approach to the Christian life will not do. We are to be the salt *of the earth* and the light *of the world*, after all. We are not salt for salt's sake, or light for light's sake, nor are we even salt or light primarily for the church's sake—we are these things for the sake of the world. Therefore, a life lived according to the

Beatitudes is one of the major ways we witness to the world. We are blessed so that we can be a blessing. The faithful citizen in Christ's kingdom knows something of the privilege that was Abraham's: "In you all the families of the earth shall be blessed" (Gen. 12:3).

It is also important to note that Jesus speaks in the plural here: "*You all* are the salt of the earth and the light of the world." It is the church, the people of God, who are to embody the principles of kingdom living and put them into practice together. The pursuit of sanctification is not like those individuals who get into their little sailboats and attempt to cross entire oceans on their own. Holiness requires the communion of saints. Sanctification is a team effort:

> And let us consider how to stir up one another to love and good works, not neglecting to meet together, as is the habit of some, but encouraging one another, and all the more as you see the Day drawing near. (Heb. 10:24–25; see also Eph. 4:17–32; Col. 3:12–17)

Likewise, it is the church whose guide is God's Word and whose goal is holy, faithful living that will bring the greatest good to the world. In what ways? How do "salty" Christians or "bright" believers bless the world? We could summarize well what Jesus is saying like this: The Christian community is most useful when it makes enticing and makes obvious the kingdom of heaven.

CHRISTIANS AS SALT

It is not uncommon to hear that salt was the primary preservative in the ancient world and that therefore Christians as "the salt of the earth" are something of a preservative agent in a decaying world. It is certainly true that our world is rotten. In fact, it is worse than decaying; it is *decayed*. It is spiritually dead. It is also true that Christians can have—and *ought* to have—a purifying, and thus preserving, effect on society. For example, it is gospel imperatives that have often compelled Christians to be the first to establish hospitals and orphanages in modern societies. This is precisely what we should expect from the believers in our midst! But is this what Jesus is conveying here with the metaphor? Likely not. Salt cannot restore meat that is already rotten, nor can Christians preserve a world that is already lost. Our hope for the world's preservation, even in the midst of her wickedness, is in God's promise: "I will never again curse the ground because of man, for the intention of man's heart is evil from his youth. Neither will I ever again strike down every living creature as I have done" (Gen. 8:21).

Therefore, in this particular instance Jesus is not referring to the preserving effects of salt as much as the flavoring effects of it. Hence, he warns "if salt has lost its taste . . ." Of the dozens of natural herbs, spices, and minerals used in cooking, none is as useful or powerful as salt. Low-sodium diets might help your blood pressure, but they do not make life more interesting. Jesus plays on the enjoyment of salt to illustrate one of the key functions of Christians in the world: We are called to draw out the rich flavor of Christ's kingdom. This means that believers are not to spice up the otherwise bland palate of a sinful world. We do not exist to make *this* world interesting. Christians are the very flavor of a *different* world entirely, the kingdom of heaven, and are thus called to be an appetizer of something so much greater than anything on the earthly menu.

The way we maintain our saltiness—which is to say, our witness—is by remaining distinct from the world. One way of applying this teaching, and a particularly important one, is to consider our speech. We must sound different from the rest of the world. That's what Paul teaches in Colossians:

Walk in wisdom toward outsiders, making the best use of the time. *Let your speech always be gracious, seasoned with salt,* so that you may know how you ought to answer each person. (Col. 4:5–6)

Our words are inextricably linked to our witness. Do the things we say pique people's interest in our Lord? Or do we have nothing different to say from anyone else? We do, of course! And that something different is nothing less than God's grace. "Let no corrupting talk come out of your mouths, but only such as is good for building up, as fits the occasion, that it may give grace to those who hear" (Eph. 4:29).

What makes us distinct is not only our speech; it's our entire character. Jesus already described this attractive distinction in the eight beatitudes of Matthew 5:3–12. If we lose the character portrayed there, then our conduct in this world will have no purpose. But if we pursue the paradoxical life of blessing—spiritual poverty, meekness, peacemaking—we actually can be useful to a lost world. Peter echoes what Jesus says here in Matthew 5:16 when he urges holy conduct for the express purpose of drawing others to the glories of God's kingdom:

> Beloved, I urge you as sojourners and exiles to abstain from the passions of the flesh, which wage war against your soul. Keep your conduct among the Gentiles honorable, so that when they speak against you as evildoers, they may see your good deeds and glorify God on the day of visitation. (1 Peter 2:11–12)

Rosaria Butterfield powerfully recounts her transformation from secularism and sexual immorality to Christianity in *The Secret Thoughts of an Unlikely Convert*. Though she doesn't use the term, her initial draw to the faith had entirely to do with a Christian being worth his salt (pardon the pun). Sitting at the dinner table with Ken and Floy Smith, Rosaria described her first appetizer of the kingdom of heaven:

> The most memorable part of this meal was Ken's prayer before the meal. I had never heard anyone pray to God as if God cared, as if God listened, and as if God answered. It was not a pretentious prayer uttered for the heathen at the table to overhear. (I have heard a few of those at gay pride marches or in front of Planned Parenthood clinics.) It was a private and honest utterance, and I felt as though I was treading on something real, something sincere, something important, and something transparent but illegible to me.[2]

This initial meal with the Smiths made Rosaria eager for more. The Lord had used something in the Smiths to make her thirsty—and notice that it was not persuasion but simple piety. Christians being Christians can and will be used by God to revolutionize the lives of the unconverted. May we never lose our saltiness. May we always be different, distinct, and thereby delightful for a needy world.

CHRISTIANS AS LIGHT

The metaphor of light also speaks to the ways God uses his people to benefit the society around them. To be light means that Christians have a mission of illumination: We are called to

---

2. Rosaria Champagne Butterfield, *The Secret Thoughts of an Unlikely Convert: An English Professor's Journey into Christian Faith*, expanded ed. (Crown and Covenant, 2014), 10.

make clear to a world lost in the darkness of ignorance who God is and what he requires of us. Butterfield said that Pastor Smith's prayer was interesting to her but also "illegible"—she still needed further explanation, instruction, and discipleship. She still needed someone to shine a light and lead her out of the dark paths of sin. We are called to both attract people *and* inform them. We are to shed light on both the true knowledge of the gospel and the holy life its message demands.³

How do we do this holistic work of illumination? The first thing to stress is that, from one perspective, we don't. We can't. Such is the stupefying power of sin that no human could ever illuminate the mind of the spiritually ignorant.

> Now this I say and testify in the Lord, that you must no longer walk as the Gentiles do, in the futility of their minds. They are darkened in their understanding, alienated from the life of God because of the ignorance that is in them, due to their hardness of heart. (Eph. 4:17–18)

Similarly, in 2 Corinthians Paul describes the condition of the lost like this: "The god of this world has blinded the minds of the unbelievers, to keep them from seeing the light of the gospel of the glory of Christ" (4:4). The only way to pierce this kind of darkness is for God himself to tear down the veils and let in the light. Conversion takes place when "God, who said, 'Let light shine out of darkness,' [shines] in our hearts to give the light of the knowledge of the glory of God in the face of Jesus Christ" (4:6). In Scripture,

---

3. Says William Hendriksen, light "means *true knowledge of the gospel* when it refers to the mind . . . it means *holiness* when it refers to the heart . . . and it means *joy, gladness,* when it refers to the emotions." William Hendriksen, *The Sermon on the Mount* (Eerdmans, 1934), 65. Emphasis original.

to wander in darkness is tantamount to spiritual death, and only God is able to raise the dead to life.

So, if the light must come from God, then what *does* it mean for us to be "the light of the world"? It means that we are a *reflected* light. Though Jesus is no longer in the world, his light still is. Through the witness of his disciples, the light of Christ yet shines upon a dark world and effects powerful change. Christians are like the moon. Even when the sun is not out, its light still shines through the luminescence of the moon. Likewise, now that Christ has ascended into glory, he calls us to reflect into the world the light of the knowledge of his glory. Another way to think of it is that Christians are like a lightbulb: We have the potential to shine, but we also have no ability to do so unless we're attached to a source of power. Christ is the energy, the power, that enables us to shine. He is Light itself; we are "light in the Lord . . . children of light" (Eph. 5:8).

This means that we can never obey the teaching of the Sermon on the Mount if we are not united to Jesus Christ. We can never live faithfully in a faithless world if we are not united to the Faithful One. The start of all obedience and all witness is resting in and receiving Jesus Christ. There is no way to shine if we have no source. And once we have him, the command is simply to let *his* glory shine through us: "Let your light—*that is, the light that has been gifted to you in and through Christ*—shine before others."

Therefore, the distinct theme that emerges here is that of *conspicuousness*. The Christian community is to be like a city on a hill that cannot be hidden, like a candle that cannot be snuffed out, like a spotlight that points people to the one true God. Christians hiding in conclaves can't be the light of the world. Christians who keep silent at the workplace in the face of injustice or evil policies are not shining their light. Churches that refuse to preach the gospel with all its implications have lost their lampstand. Our character and conduct must not only *interest* people (salt) but also *inform* them (light). In the Bible, light is connected with revelation. We must be prepared to reflect the light of Christ's revelation when we speak, instruct, refute, and proclaim.

We not only tell of the Lord but also live for him: "Let your light shine before others, so that they may see your good works and give glory to your Father who is in heaven." Our good works are not means of building our own brand or flaunting our own righteousness. Our good works are first and foremost *God's* good works (see Eph. 2:10). When we do good works, we are simply showing and sharing and telling what the Lord has done in our lives. This will draw people to *him*, not to us. It will be a means by which people learn of *his* kingdom: what conduct must be left behind and what new conduct must be taken up. We should answer the call of the Prophets: "O house of Jacob, come, let us walk in the light of the Lord" (Isa. 2:5).

CONCLUSION

The way we are to influence the world according to these two metaphors is directly related to the kind of character we are called to in the Beatitudes. Before we can expect to be used by God to bring about change in this world, we ourselves need to be changed. Many Christians talk about transforming the culture while giving little thought to the need of their own inner transformation. Without it, our attempts to influence the culture may very well lead to it looking more like us, but not necessarily looking more like Christ (see Rom. 12:1–2). So, the order here is key: The Beatitudes come first; salt and light are a consequence.

Inevitably, we will at times doubt that God could be up to anything good or useful through this call to ordinary faithfulness, whether it's for us or for others. We are prone to discouragement and disillusionment. Since we can't figure out the paradoxical puzzle that weakness is greatness, we are tempted to give up on the idea altogether. And while the devil loves to tell us that our efforts in the Christian life are a whopping waste of time and effort, let Jesus's voice be heard louder. He even repeats himself so we don't forget it: "Blessed are... Blessed are... Blessed are..." *This*, and no other, is the path to true blessing.

Let me offer two concluding encouragements as you set out on it, whether for the first time or the umpteenth time. First, be encouraged that God knows how to care for the world that he has made and advance the kingdom that he has established. Whether it makes sense to us or not, *this* is the path for faithful witness in a crumbling culture. Will it bring about revolutionary change? Maybe. Maybe not. But what we should have our sights set on, more than a glorious revolution, is the glory of God. Jesus shows us how to please God here, and he tells us explicitly in John: "By this my Father is glorified, that you bear much fruit and so prove to be my disciples" (15:8). May we all, therefore, set our sights as high as holiness. May God make us as holy as saints on this side of glory can be, and as useful as would bring him honor.

Second, be encouraged that when you do live this way, it will never be in vain. That's been a primary message that Jesus preaches in the Beatitudes: The Christian life is not a waste. Do you spend your days hungering after righteousness? You will be filled. Your longing will not be for nothing. Do you desire God above all others, loving him with heart, soul, mind, and strength? Then you will actually get him. Do you seek for the hidden joy in the midst of persecution? Then you will be greatly rewarded! Whatever we have to put in to achieve the life described here, we will get out much more. Let us follow him today, tomorrow, and every day—we won't be disappointed.

FOR FURTHER REFLECTION

1. What is the relationship between the final verses considered in this chapter and the beatitudes that preceded them?
2. We are blessed in order to be a blessing. How does this fact reshape the way we interpret the Beatitudes?
3. What is the meaning of "salt of the earth"? What does it mean to be the "light of the world"? How could you live out this calling in this very week?
4. "Weakness is greatness" is a paradoxical puzzle that we are tempted to give up on. How can embracing this paradox—that our efforts in ordinary faithfulness are never in vain and will yield abundant returns—combat discouragement and disillusionment in the Christian life?
5. Considering the overall message of *Paradox People*, what is one significant way your perspective on Christian living has been challenged or deepened by the exploration of the Beatitudes in this book?

ACKNOWLEDGMENTS

As with any book, many more people come together to make it possible than the one whose name is on the front cover. First thanks goes to Dave Almack of P&R, who invited me to a conversation with him about what book subjects could be useful for Christians today. That discussion landed us on the Beatitudes, but it was at least a year before I even attempted to put to pen to paper. He never wavered in his support throughout the whole process. Amanda Martin, Elizabeth Holmlund, and the rest of the editorial team worked tirelessly on this project. The whole crew at P&R have been great to work with (again!), and I thank them for their labors.

My good friend Neil Quinn read over several chapters, and you will know which ones they are, since they are better than the rest. His editorial suggestions were immensely helpful. The feedback I received from Craig Troxel—generously offered during a busy grading period for him—was likewise used to make this material stronger. I also wish to thank Philip Poots, a colleague and friend, who encouraged me in my writing and offered helpful edits, as well as the intrepid Ryan McGraw, who proved to be a very close and attentive reader. My wife, Kerri Ann, not only supported me in the process but also served as a great sounding board—and even as an editor for several chapters. Her insight on the subject of Christian living is just one of the many reasons I married her.

Acknowledgments

I also wish to thank my congregation, Community Presbyterian Church in Kalamazoo, Michigan, who listened to this material in early form during our midweek studies. They were attentive, they gave good feedback, and they encouraged me in my teaching ministry. It's one thing to write about the Christian life. It's quite another to teach and preach on it to people with whom you actually live the Christian life. The former would be an exercise in rhetoric; the latter is an exercise in sanctification. I am thankful for such wonderful saints with whom I can experience kingdom blessings.

I am especially grateful that I do not minister in the kingdom alone. God has seen fit to bless me with many pastoral friends and mentors who spur me on in my own calling. One of those is the aforementioned Neil Quinn, pastor of Good Shepherd Presbyterian Church, which is about four blocks from my own congregation. Neil and I came to Kalamazoo at around the same time. I was revitalizing a church; he was planting one. I view Neil with nothing less than admiration and respect. He is a dear brother to me, and I wish to be more like him—particularly as he embodies the kingdom character our Lord commends here. Neil loves the ways of God and helps me to love them too. If you are ever in Kalamazoo, you should visit his church and see what I mean. With thanks for his friendship and partnership in the gospel, and glory to God for how many he has helped enter the kingdom of heaven, I dedicate this book to him.